The Art of Collaboration

THE BIG AMERICANS

The Art of Collaboration

THE BIG AMERICANS

Jane Kinsman

■ national gallery of australia

Produced by the Publications Department of the National Gallery of Australia, Canberra

www.nga.gov.au

Designer: Beverly Swifte
Printer: PMP Limited
Prepress: Showads Melbourne

Cataloguing-in-Publication data
Kinsman, Jane.
The art of collaboration : the big Americans.

ISBN 0 642 54154 X.

1. Prints, American. 2. Prints - 20th century – United States.
I. National Gallery
of Australia. II. Title.

769.973

Distributed in Australia by
Thames and Hudson
11 Central Boulevard Business Park
Port Melbourne, Victoria 3207

Distributed in the United Kingdom by
Thames and Hudson
181A High Holborn
London WC1V 7QX, UK

Distributed in the United States of America by
University of Washington Press
1326 Fifth Avenue, Ste 555
Seattle, WA 98101-2604

This publication accompanies the exhibition *The Big Americans: Albers, Frankenthaler, Hockney, Johns, Lichtenstein, Motherwell, Rauschenberg and Stella at Tyler's studios* at the National Gallery of Australia, Canberra, 4 October 2002 – 27 January 2003, Curator Jane Kinsman, National Gallery of Australia.

(cover)
Roy LICHTENSTEIN
Nude with Blue Hair (detail)
colour relief print from the series *Nudes* 1994
published by Tyler Graphics Ltd, Mount Kisco, New York
Purchased with the assistance of the Orde Poynton Fund 2002

Acknowledgements
I would like to thank the Chairman, Harold Mitchell, and members of the National Gallery of Australia Council, the Director, Dr Brian Kennedy, and all my friends and colleagues at the National Gallery for their generous support for this publication and the accompanying exhibition.

My sincere thanks go to Kenneth Tyler, Marabeth Cohen-Tyler and the staff at Tyler Graphics Ltd, Mount Kisco, for their untiring assistance and generosity. To the artists or their foundations, a special thanks for the provision of information and assistance in copyright matters. For marvellous inclusions to the exhibition I would like to thank the following lenders: David Hockney; John Hockney; John Kaldor; the Museum of Contemporary Art, Sydney; Harry and Penelope Seidler; Charles Simonyi; Frank Stella; and Ken and Marabeth Tyler.

Special thanks to Pauline Green and Beverly Swifte who have made such an important contribution to this publication.

Jane Kinsman
Senior Curator International Prints, Drawings and Illustrated Books
National Gallery of Australia
September 2002

In memory of my husband Terry Counihan

Contents

(above) Frank Stella studies a proof of *Monstrous Pictures of Whales* as Kenneth Tyler
pulls an impression from the press, 1993 (photograph Jim McHugh).

Foreword

The National Gallery of Australia has had a long and special relationship with the wonderful master printer, Kenneth Tyler. It was one of the inspired decisions of the first Director of the Gallery, James Mollison (in the same year that Jackson Pollock's *Blue Poles* was acquired) to work with Tyler to bring to Canberra a most remarkable collection of right-to-print proofs and other related material. This represented all the work that Tyler had been doing on the west coast of America between 1966 and 1973. He then moved across to the east coast, and the Gallery, through its continuing collaboration with him, has now acquired the most extraordinary collection of material, establishing it as one of the great repositories of postwar American prints.

Ken Tyler's ambition has always been to make great prints by working with great artists. His brilliance as a printer, and his strength and influence as a colleague and friend of so many superb artists, has been attested by the artists themselves in generous acknowledgment. He is a magician, conjuring the best of possibilities into reality in print. Frank Stella has remarked that Tyler pushes the technique in ways that can't really be seen, because it is just those little things that make all the difference. This master printer has raised printmaking to a supreme art form.

The remarkable complexity of the prints produced at Ken Tyler's workshops is borne out in the description of the extraordinary mural print that resulted from his wonderful collaboration with Frank Stella: *The Fountain* is a 67-colour, hand-coloured woodcut, etching, aquatint, relief, drypoint, screenprint, on three sheets of natural kozo fibre handmade paper, with seven screenprinted natural gampi fibre handmade paper collage elements.

Spanning 231.1cm in height by 700.4cm in length. It was derived from an original collage, and printed from three carved woodblocks and 105 intaglio plates.

This publication about the art of collaboration recognises Ken Tyler's involvement with some of the great artists of recent times, and also with the National Gallery of Australia. We are proud and honoured to have worked with him, and we are very grateful for his sensitivity and his generosity of spirit.

Much of the success of the Gallery's involvement with Ken Tyler is due to his friendship and respect for Jane Kinsman, our Senior Curator of International Prints, Drawings and Illustrated Books. Having a scholar who has the respect of pivotal figures in the contemporary art world is of great benefit to an institution such as ours. The acquisition of the Tyler print archive by the National Gallery of Australia will stand as a testament to the curatorial skill of Jane Kinsman, and the support given by the Gallery's Council. I pay tribute to former Chairman, Kerry Stokes, AO, and current Chairman, Harold Mitchell, and their respective Councils, for supporting the Gallery's efforts to build on the strengths of our collection. This requires commitment, courage and dedication, just the attributes which allowed Ken Tyler to achieve pre-eminent status in his profession.

Dr Brian Kennedy
Director
National Gallery of Australia

The Art of Collaboration
Introduction

'As a printmaker and publisher I can only be as successful as the artists I work with and the art we create together.'[1] Kenneth Tyler was referring to his collaborations with David Hockney, but his comments would apply equally to the select group of talented artists who have benefited from the creative environment of the various Tyler print workshops from the 1960s to the present day.

For Tyler, collaboration with these artists engages both heart and mind; it inspires innovation, response and reaction. The printer has to be like a chameleon, changing in disposition and approach to suit a particular artist's temperament and needs. Collaboration also requires a degree of selflessness on the part of the printer and the workshop team — the artist comes first. Frank Stella has observed that Tyler is 'more driven than the artists he works with, he won't go home before you do, he's always there — and in the end he's always there for you.'[2]

THE COLLECTION

The success of the collaboration between this master printer and key artists on the American art scene is manifestly evident in the National Gallery of Australia's collection of editioned original prints, screens, paper works, illustrated books and multiples, along with rare and unique proofs and drawings produced at Tyler's workshops — on the east coast, at Gemini Ltd and Gemini GEL in Los Angeles (established 1965 and 1966); and on the west coast in New York state, at Tyler Workshop Ltd, Bedford Village (1974), and Tyler Graphics Ltd at Bedford Village (1975) and Mount Kisco (1987).

The seeds of the collection were sown in 1973 when the National Gallery acquired some some 600 prints, rare proofs and related drawings from Tyler. After the arrival

(opposite) **Josef ALBERS Homage to the Square: On an Early Sky** 1964 oil on composition board

of this rich assembly, a policy of purchase (formalised by the Gallery in 1982) has seen the continued acquisition of works from Tyler's studios. With a recent major gift and purchase, this collection has been augmented to form a significant repository of the work produced at the Tyler workshops by foremost artists of the contemporary period.[3]

The collection documents an extraordinary story of artist and printer collaboration in postwar America. Amongst many others, artists of such international standing as Josef Albers, Helen Frankenthaler, David Hockney, Jasper Johns, Roy Lichtenstein, Robert Motherwell, Robert Rauschenberg and Frank Stella have produced some of their finest works in a workshop atmosphere that celebrates creativity. While each artist brings their individual talents and ideas to the studio, Tyler is able not only to facilitate, but also to extend the possibilities available to them.

The remarkable story of Tyler's print workshops should be seen in the context of historical developments in printmaking in Europe and postwar America.

A BURST OF COLOUR

The process of printing from a lithographic stone was discovered at the close of the eighteenth century by a Bavarian, Alois Senefelder, who with his business partner, Johann Anton André, promoted the technique, first as a means of reproducing sheet music. The history of lithography over the following century was one of fluctuating fashion and disfavour. In other German states and in England and France, artists were encouraged to adopt the process as a means of making their drawings in multiple form. For example, German artists Wilhelm Reuter and Karl Friedrich Schinkel embraced the technique, as did Benjamin West, Henry Fuseli and other noted British Academicians, along with major French artists, among them Théodore Géricault and Eugène Delacroix. In 1817 Senefelder had begun experimenting with colour, and two decades later Godefroy Engelmann patented his 'chromolithographic' process. In 1837, two years after the German patent, Charles Hullmandel, in England, developed a system of colour tints which were used, for example, for the scenic views by Thomas Shotter Boys. By the mid-nineteenth century colour lithography had fallen into disrepute; it had come to be associated with cheap, poor quality, mass produced printings, and many artists shunned the use of colour. The process flowered again in the late nineteenth century when the more avant-garde artists returned to the use of colour lithography. Technical advances allowed for work on a large scale; and postermaking was transformed from merely an instrument of advertising to an art form in its own right when artists such as Pierre Bonnard, Henri de Toulouse-Lautrec and Alphonse Mucha were drawn to the medium.

For the artist the advent of lithography meant immediate involvement, drawing directly onto the stone. The complexity of the lithographic process, however, more than any other printing technique, meant that an artist relied heavily on the printer's expertise. Lithography therefore encouraged collaboration between artist and printer.

In the twentieth century lithography experienced a chequered history. In postwar America it floundered because printers were not embracing change, and

Jasper Johns using scotch stone to create lithographic cancellation proof for *No*, Gemini GEL, 1969 (photograph William Crutchfield)

could not attract artists of quality. In 1959 the artist June Wayne submitted a grant proposal to the director of the Ford Foundation's program in humanities and the arts, W. McNeil Lowry, to establish the Tamarind Lithography Workshop. The art of lithography was in a particularly parlous state; Wayne saw it as an endangered species.

In my mind, lithography has been linked to the great white whooping crane, which like lithography, was on the verge of extinction when the Tamarind workshop came into being. In all the world there were only thirty-six whooping cranes left; and in the United States there were no master printers able to work with the creative spectrum of our artists.

The artist/lithographers, like the cranes, needed a protected environment and a concerned public so that, once rescued from extinction, they could make a go of it on their own. If lithography could be revived, all the print media would benefit — as indeed they did. And the Tamarind 'preserve' could become a model for other art forms — as indeed it has.[4]

Whatever skills remained in the postwar period had to be nurtured, the technical know-how preserved and passed on. Artists had to be enticed back to working with lithography, to again consider it as an art form. To June Wayne's astonishment, the Ford Foundation agreed to her proposal, and funding was provided to establish the Tamarind Lithography Workshop in Los Angeles, California, in 1960, co-founded with Clinton Adams. The workshop moved to Albuquerque, New Mexico, in 1970. This institution became an important instrument in what has sometimes been dubbed the American print renaissance. Subsequently, many talented artists and printers honed their skills at Tamarind. It was a place where quality and technical skill took pride of place, the workshop's educational role was also a prime focus. Expertise in lithography came to be widely disseminated with many Tamarind-trained lithographers working in the field.

KEN TYLER AT TAMARIND
Ken Tyler studied at the Art Institute of Chicago and the John Herron School of Art, Indianapolis. Then in 1963, he was given a Ford Foundation Fellowship to work at the

Roy Lichtenstein cutting *Roommates* Rubylith stencil, 1994, Tyler Graphics Ltd, Mount Kisco (photograph Marabeth Cohen-Tyler)

Tamarind Lithography Workshop. His first task was to work on ink and plate research and exclusively collaborate with Josef Albers on his lithographs, in a private studio set up next to the workshop. He also made regular contributions to the technical information on metal plate and chemistry for the *Tamarind Book of Lithography* published in 1971 and co-authored by Garo Antreasian and Clinton Adams. At Tamarind he also studied under Marcel Durassier, the French master printer. Durassier was noted for his technical skill and had worked at the French lithography workshop, Mourlot Frères, with some of the great artists of the School of Paris, including Picasso and Miró.

Durassier understood the demands of working in lithography, once describing it as a 'stubborn old goat' — Tyler noted that this could also be said of Durassier himself. 'Marcel was a difficult man', Tyler recently recalled, 'but not with me. He gave me his roller the first week at Tamarind and made me his apprentice. Learned a great deal from him. Most of all his rub-up technique for stone lithography, which I have practised with great success over the years.'[5] It was Durassier's belief that, no matter what the imagery, the printer should always provide the artist with the very best technical expertise. This attitude had a profound effect on Tyler. His experience at Tamarind allowed him to develop skills, through research and practice, which earned him a reputation for technical wizardry, and he became a notable player in the development of printmaking in America. A brilliant and creative technician, Tyler was to become the technical director of Tamarind in 1964–65.

GROSMAN AND UNIVERSAL LIMITED ART EDITIONS

Another key figure in American postwar printmaking was Russian-born Tatyana Grosman, who established the workshop Universal Limited Art Editions (ULAE) in West Islip on Long Island, New York, in 1957. It was Grosman's goal to develop a studio for fine art lithography (later an etching studio was added), and she was particularly interested in the *livre d'artiste* (the artist's book). *Livres d'artiste* had their origins in nineteenth-century France, with artists not simply illustrating a text, but contributing inspired imagery that was the creative equal of the text. One of the formative examples was the deluxe edition of Edgar Allan Poe's *Le Corbeau [The raven]* (Paris: Richard Lesclide, 1875), where Edouard Manet's dark compositions were combined with the powerful imagery of the verse. The Paris art dealer and publisher Ambroise Vollard furthered this idea at the beginning of the twentieth century, producing luxury books of great beauty. Vollard and a number of other publishers oversaw the production of limited editions of exquisite original prints on beautiful papers, where image and text were treated as harmonious components of carefully laid out pages.

It was such an approach that Grosman aspired to, and she continued this tradition with her commitment to fine printing, high quality papers, inks and materials. Grosman's persuasive manner and the atmosphere of her workshop encouraged many artists to work at ULAE. For Robert Motherwell it was 'her integrity, tenacity, endless patience, extravagance with time and materials … as rare as is the ambience of her workshops, where it is simply assumed … that the world of the spirit exists as concretely as, say, lemon yellow or woman's hair'.[6] ULAE had a delightful air of amateurism about it. It was like 'somebody had found a press and opened a shop in a garage'.[7] Indeed, that was the case. Luck also played a part — the first lithographic stones were discovered in the pathway leading to the Grosmans' modest house adjoining the studio.

Tatyana Grosman had a fine critical sense and a great awareness of her materials, but not a deep technical understanding of the printing processes. When she established ULAE, she felt that the printer should just begin in the morning and whatever was printed that day would be the edition. She believed that each day the circumstances of the printer and the environment in which the printing took place changed, so if an edition continued on another day, it would look different. In contrast, the Tamarind workshop's approach was more oriented to mass production; different artists arrived every month and the technique of lithography was the dominant concern, over and above the art that was produced.

Grosman was not particularly interested in the notion of collaboration between the artist and the printer. It was up to the printer to solve problems.[8] 'The way we work is very simple', she said in an interview for *The New Yorker* in 1976, 'the artist makes his drawing on the stone, the printer makes a proof, and then the artist decides what he likes or doesn't like, and makes changes, and maybe I make some suggestions, and we select the paper,

Kenneth Tyler pins sheets of acetate in registration as David Hockney draws and paints on them for *Caribbean Tea Time*, 1987 (photograph Lindsay Green)

The main press room at Tyler Graphics Ltd during Helen Frankenthaler's *Reflections* project, 1995. Kenneth Tyler, on the right, is inking a roller in preparation for applying ink to the lithographic stone (photograph Marabeth Cohen-Tyler)

and that's how it is.'[9] She established a small 'family' of artists who were invited to work at West Islip. Belonging to a generation earlier than Tyler's, she pursued many of America's Abstract Expressionist artists. Most of them were not interested in printmaking and had little understanding of the beautiful book philosophy — outstanding exceptions, such as Robert Motherwell and Helen Frankenthaler, both produced important editions at ULAE.

THE TYLER WORKSHOPS

After his Tamarind experience, and now keen to be an independent player and sufficiently 'desperate' to 'gamble everything', in September 1965, aged in his early thirties, Tyler established his own print workshop in Los Angeles, Gemini Ltd — 'a modest backroom space rented from Jerry Solomon's frame shop'.[10] A few months later, in January 1966, with partners Stanley Grinstein and Sidney B. Felsen, he established the fine print publishing house Gemini GEL (Graphic Editions Ltd), with the intention of publishing state-of-the-art prints. Discussing the change

with artist Josef Albers, Tyler explained that Gemini GEL was a publishing house as well as a print workshop — where his partners allowed him the freedom to do the things he wanted to do.[11] In a lecture at the University of Southern California in 1965, the Museum of Modern Art's William Lieberman had 'shocked' Tyler by stating the obvious: that great art is made by great artists. The message for Tyler was that 'great prints are made only by great artists'.[12] With this in mind he set out to ensnare the very best artists of his day, with the promise, 'Here is a workshop, there are no rules, no restrictions, do what you want to do.'[13] He took inspiration also from Picasso's methods of printmaking, where the rule book was thrown out; otherwise, as Tyler has noted, 'if you have all these "can'ts" in there, you change the nature of creativity'.[14] Gemini GEL, Tyler Workshop Ltd and Tyler Graphics Ltd achieved their outstanding reputation because of this philosophy and Tyler's belief in the infinite possibilities of printmaking and the art of collaboration.

Notes
1. Ken Tyler, 'Layers of Space and Time: David Hockney's *Moving Focus*', in *Contemporary Master Prints from the Lilja Collection*, Liechtenstein and London: the Lilja Art Fund Foundation in association with Azimuth Editions Limited, 1995, p. 125.
2. Frank Stella, Qantas Birthday Lecture, 13 October 1999, National Gallery of Australia, Canberra.
3. Other major collections of prints produced at the Tyler workshops are housed at the Walker Art Center, Minneapolis, USA, the Centre for Contemporary Graphic Art, Fukushima, Japan, and the Singapore Art Museum.
4. Lucinda H. Gedeon (ed.), *June Wayne: a retrospective*, New York: Neuberger Museum of Art, Purchase College, State University of New York, 1997, p. 42.
5. Ken Tyler, correspondence with Jane Kinsman, 17 June 2002.
6. Stephanie Terenzio (ed.), *The Collected Writings of Robert Motherwell*, New York: Oxford University Press, 1992, p. 213.
7. Ben Berns, in Stephanie Terenzio, *The Prints of Robert Motherwell* (catalogue raisonné by Dorothy C. Belknap), New York: Hudson Hills Press, 1991, p. 49.
8. Tatyana Grosman, in Stephanie Terenzio, *The Prints of Robert Motherwell* (catalogue raisonné by Dorothy C. Belknap), New York: Hudson Hills Press, 1991, p. 56.
9. Calvin Tomkins, 'Profiles: the moods of stone', *The New Yorker*, 1 June 1976, p. 45.
10. Ken Tyler, 'Layers of Space and Time: David Hockney's *Moving Focus*', in *Contemporary Master Prints from the Lilja Collection*, Liechtenstein and London: the Lilja Art Fund Foundation in association with Azimuth Editions Limited, 1995, p. 121.
11. Ken Tyler, transcript of undated telephone call with Josef Albers, 1966, copy held by Jane Kinsman.
12. Ken Tyler, in *Reaching Out: Ken Tyler, master printer* (documentary film), Avery Tirce Productions, 1976.
13. ibid..
14. Pat Gilmour, 'Ken Tyler and the Limitless Possibilities of Collaborative Printmaking', in *Innovation in Collaborative Printmaking: Kenneth Tyler 1963–1992* (exhibition catalogue), Tokyo: the Yomiuri Shimbun, 1992, p. 17.

The Art of Seduction
Josef Albers, Robert Rauschenberg and Jasper Johns

From the very beginning Ken Tyler sought to collaborate with some of the postwar greats in the American art scene. He first set his sights on the German-born émigré, Josef Albers, an artist obsessed with form and colour since his days at the Bauhaus. In 1920 Albers had responded to the call of the Bauhaus manifesto, proclaimed by its first director, Walter Gropius: Come back to the guild; come back to hand work. And at the age of 32 Albers, an artist and teacher in the traditional mould, became a student at the Weimar Bauhaus: 'I threw all my old things out the window.'[1]

When the Bauhaus moved to the Gropius- and school-designed complex at Dessau in 1925, Albers was made a master of the school. Following the rise of the National Socialists, he migrated with the Bauhaus to Berlin in 1932 and stayed until the school's demise in 1933. Albers now had to make another decision that would change his life and, with his Jewish wife the artist Anni Albers, he left Germany for America at the behest of the architect Philip Johnson, who proposed he accept a teaching post at Black Mountain College, North Carolina. The importance of Albers the artist and teacher and proselytiser of theories on colour and vision, and his influence on the following generation of artists, has received appropriate recognition in recent years, including a major retrospective at the Solomon R. Guggenheim Museum in New York in 1988.

Albers was 75 when he met Tyler at the Tamarind Lithography Workshop in Los Angeles where both were granted fellowships in 1963. While at Tamarind, the artist and the printer worked on two series of Albers prints, *Day & Night: Homage to the Square* and *Midnight and Noon.*[2]

Josef ALBERS
from the series *White Line Squares* 1966 colour lithographs
(opposite and right) **White Line Square I, III, VI**

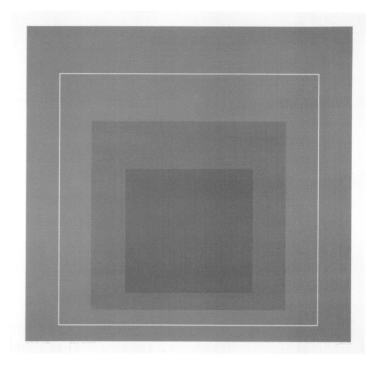

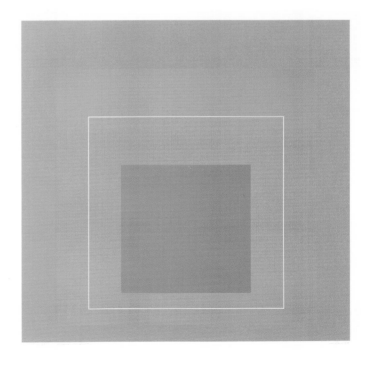

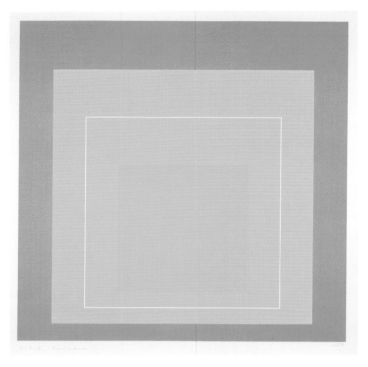
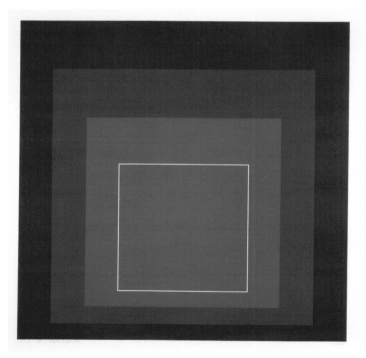
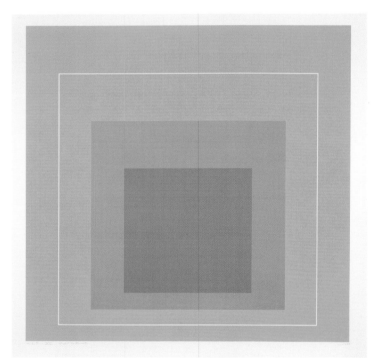

Josef ALBERS
from the series *White Line Squares* 1966
colour lithographs (left to right above and below)
White Line Square IX–XII

8

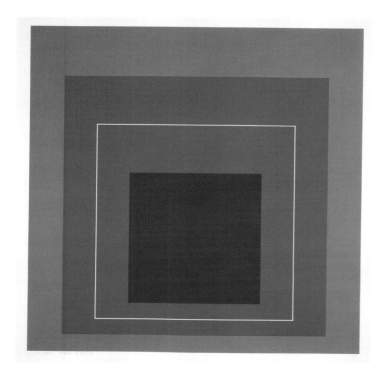

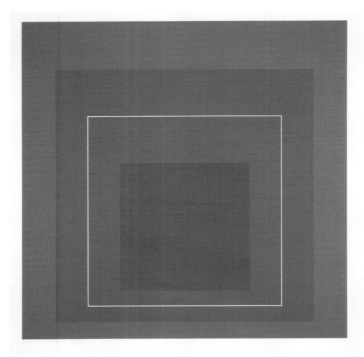

Josef ALBERS
from the series *White Line Squares* 1966
colour lithographs (left to right above and below)
White Line Square XIII–XVI

9

Initially, Albers had been sceptical about using lithography; he believed the process could not match the luminosity that he achieved in his painting series *Homage to the Square*. These paintings, which he began in 1950 and continued to work on obsessively for the rest of his life, consisted of what Albers called 'platters to serve color' — in different combinations, because of their interactions, the colours would have different 'readings'.[3] Working with Albers at Tamarind, Tyler experimented with thinning the inks and blotting the printed surface, which brought a new subtlety to the colours which was pleasing to the artist.

Soon after the establishment of Gemini GEL in January 1966, Tyler contacted Albers, proposing that they work together on a series of lithographs — which became the seminal *White Line Squares*. The technical problems of obtaining perfect registration was something Tyler had mulled over for some time and he was able to promise Albers that there would be no accidental printing of one colour over another, which would have distorted the artist's carefully selected colours. The exercise required that a perfect fine white line be created; this would be achieved by leaving the white paper exposed without any bleeding of the inks.

The series was initially produced as two sets of eight colour lithographs, with a subsequent 17th print. Both series were issued in 1966. The series became the visual expression of Albers' thesis:

A white line within a color area instead of as a contour may present a newly discovered effect: When the line is placed within a so-called 'Middle' color, even when the color is very evenly applied, it will make the one color look like two different shades or tints of that color.[4]

The result is the appearance of four colours, despite the use of only three inks.

This initial collaborative venture of Tyler's Gemini GEL workshop is a *tour de force* of colour lithography, but it took many months to achieve the perfect result. Tyler

(opposite) Joseph Albers and Kenneth Tyler, 1974, Tyler Graphics Ltd, Bedford Village (photograph Renate Ponsold Motherwell)

visited Albers at his New Haven, Connecticut, home to discuss the idea, then returned to Los Angeles. Thereafter, Albers sent back to the workshop detailed instructions and colour samples in the post. Telephone calls continued the process, in which the artist commented on the proofing, analysing what worked and what didn't. Further proofing followed until Albers was perfectly satisfied. The samples and proofs with the notations of Albers and Tyler now housed at the National Gallery of Australia attest the infinite care taken by both artist and printer in their collaborative effort.

In a three-way discussion with Henry Hopkins, of the Los Angeles County Museum, and Tyler in 1966, Albers described to Hopkins their method of working, admitting: 'I never touch the stone, never the rule, never the ink, it's all done by my friend Ken, but I watch him like Hell.'[5] Such an approach brought criticism from certain quarters. The American Print Council had published *What Is an Original Print?* by Theodore Gusten in 1961, in which Gusten insisted that artists had to work directly on the matrix themselves for a print to be considered original. Albers complained to Tyler: Gusten 'thinks you should make the plate as the woodcutter of the old style did'; and he observed that Dürer had not cut even one of his plates.[6]

Gusten's opinion was also at odds with the views of the noted curator of prints at France's Bilbiothèque Nationale, Jean Adhémar, and the French printer–publisher Fernand Mourlot. Both recognised that an artist may not always draw directly on the lithographic stone or plate because of the technical complexities involved, and that printers and chromistes would sometimes have to convert the designs of the artist into a printable form. 'I fully share his opinion', Mourlot wrote of Adhémar, that 'if the artist was present at the making of his lithograph, even if he didn't do it entirely himself, if he approved it, if he did his corrections, if he agreed to the printing, followed the proofing and signed the lithograph, it is an original lithograph.'[7]

The American Print Council failed to recognise the necessity of collaboration between artist and printer, criticising Tyler and Albers for their efforts at Tamarind.

Such a view could not be sustained. Reflecting on the council's role, Tyler noted recently: 'By the end of the 60s one never heard about the Print Council.'[8]

Albers became both a friend and a mentor to Tyler and he assisted the workshop by donating some four-fifths of the proceeds of the sale of *White Line Squares* to fund future projects. Prints from the series became Tyler's calling cards and he took the set when he visited artists on his wish list. He regarded these prints as the 'first notes on the piano'; 'whatever symphony was to follow was because of them'.[9] This 'symphony' of extraordinary innovation, scale and technical virtuosity forms the Tyler collection at the National Gallery of Australia.

CALLING CARDS

Another artist who was enticed to work at Gemini GEL early in 1966 was Robert Rauschenberg. He was one of a stable of emerging artists attached to the New York gallery of Leo Castelli, which also included Roy Lichtenstein, Jasper Johns, Frank Stella and Claes Oldenburg. Rauschenberg had been a student of Albers at Black Mountain College and had a deep admiration for his teacher, although their relationship had been difficult. 'Albers was a beautiful teacher and an impossible person … He wasn't easy to talk to, and I found his criticism so excruciating and so devastating that I never asked for it. Years later, though, I'm still learning what he taught me … I consider Albers the most important teacher I've ever had.'[10] 'What he taught had to do with the entire visual world.'[11]

Tyler travelled to New York in early February 1966, visiting Jasper Johns and Rauschenberg, using his calling cards to great effect.

During our meetings I showed them the Albers' White Line Squares and John Altoon prints … They were impressed with the work and it helped that Leo Castelli had already visited my small workshop and was keen for Bob (more so than for Jasper) to work with me. My take on this was that Bob was having a rougher time financially. The 'cast of players' who all knew what I was up to, were Leo [Castelli], David Whitney [who was working at the Castelli Gallery] and Philip Johnson. All very close to these two artists at the time.[12]

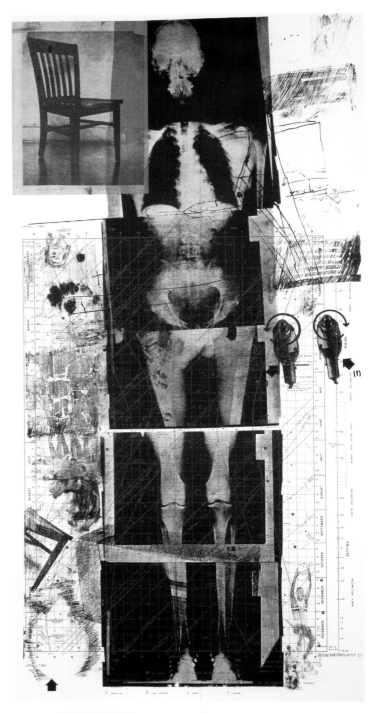

Robert RAUSCHENBERG Booster colour lithograph, screenprint
from the series *Booster and 7 Studies* 1967

For Rauschenberg Tyler's promise that scale was not a problem was assurance enough. He decided to make a life-sized self-portrait and promptly took himself off to the Kaiser Medical Group where he had himself X-rayed in the nude, except for a pair of large boots. This X-ray became the key element for the print, *Booster* 1967. Photographic elements, the artist's drawing and some rubbings helped to complete the image. The ground-breaking size of *Booster* required the use of two lithographic stones placed in the press one after the other, with the large sheet run through the press twice for the combined image. The astonishing nature of this work meant that many in the art world took notice, and Tyler began to gain a reputation as a talented master printer.

Booster became a key stepping stone in the history of postwar American printmaking, where limits to imagination and scale were discarded. It remains one of the most significant prints made in the twentieth century, helping to bring printmaking into a new era in which prints were to rival paintings in invention and size. Not all responded favourably, however. The French printer Durassier, who had taught Tyler at Tamarind and was working at Mourlot, asked why the artist had been allowed to make such a big print. Coming from a European workshop tradition, he found it incomprehensible that such leeway should be given to an artist. He criticised Tyler 'for pushing lithography past its natural scale and giving in to the artist'.[13]

What was also notable about *Booster* was the combination of the different techniques of lithography and screenprinting on mould-made paper. It was 'a first' for Tyler.

Booster was supposed to have been a lithograph — the biggest hand pulled lithograph to date — it finally needed to be silkscreened. 'The problem' … was printing an opaque grid on top of black. You can't print white or color over black with lithography. Lithography is not opaque.[14]

The combination of printing methods was a radical departure from established practice. For example, Tamarind specialised in lithography; and Crown Point Press in San Francisco, originally established as a communal workshop in 1962, specialised in etching and other intaglio techniques. Subsequently, Tyler would offer artists an almost limitless range of techniques, adding to their potential with handmade papers of a quality, shape and size never seen before. Such an approach was to be a major factor in the success of the Tyler workshops, and led to significant advances in printmaking in America.

JOY, PAIN, ECSTACY

Rauschenberg's next project with Gemini GEL was a revolutionary print series, *Stoned Moon* of 1969–70, in which the artist's aspirations and inspirations were matched by the skill and inventiveness of Tyler and the workshop team. Rauschenberg had been invited by NASA (the National Aeronautic and Space Administration) to witness the launch from the Kennedy Space Centre, Florida, of the rocket that would land a man on the moon. The artist was then commissioned by Gemini to make a series of prints drawing on this experience.

With photographs and documentation provided by NASA, Rauschenberg set himself the task of working on a series of lithographs using this material and adding his own drawing in lithographic tusche. Rauschenberg found the whole experience astounding, particularly the combination of the high-tech event with the human struggle to support the venture. This juxtaposition of technology and the everyday inspired his imagery — for example, he noticed a bird's nest perched on a NASA structure while people were carrying out their specialised tasks on the ground below. The resulting prints are almost surreal in character, with their strange combinations of recycled and reconfigured imagery.

Rauschenberg later described the strange and awe-inspiring scene of the launch.

The bird's nest bloomed with fire and clouds. Softly largely slowly silently Apollo 11 started to move up. Then it rose being lifted on light. Standing mid-air, it began to sing happily loud in its own joy wanting the earth to know it was going, saturated, super-saturated and solidified air with a sound that became your body. For that while everything was the same material. Power over power joy pain ecstasy. There was no inside, no out. Then bodily transcending a state of energy, Apollo 11 was airborne, lifting pulling everyone's spirits with it.[15]

Aside from the originality of the concept of the *Stoned Moon* series, these prints required technical inventiveness and resourcefulness; and the scale of several of the works, including *Sky Garden*, had implications for the future

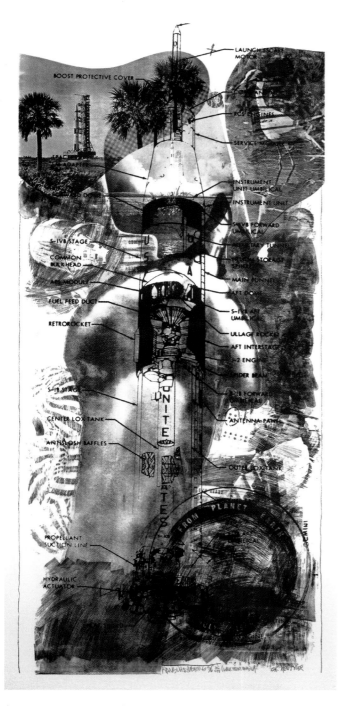

Robert RAUSCHENBERG Sky Garden 1969 colour trial proof
from *Stoned Moon* series 1969–70 colour lithograph, screenprint

everything else has to change. And of course what has to happen is that you need more than one person. It was the beginnings of what I reflect back now was the team relationship in the workshop … For Sky Garden … I laminated three stones together on some honeycomb backing and then built a press that big to print it. Each and every impression required about two pounds of ink. To wipe that stone needed four people just to keep it moist so they could roll the roller across it and traverse back and forth. That's five people, five people around a press all day, for many many days until it was done.[16]

While Tyler is the orchestrator and conductor of the orchestra, the members of his workshop are the skilled players who contribute to the success of each venture. In the case of the *Stoned Moon* series, Charles Ritt, Daniel Freeman, Andrew Vlady, Robert Peterson, Timothy Isham, Ron Adams, Timothy Hutchausen, Stuart Henderson and Ron Olds worked on the project over its duration. Experiences such as these underscore the symbiotic nature of the relationship between the artist and the workshop, necessary to achieve the most innovative work.

Artists form attachments to lithographic stones, and work well with certain printers. Rauschenberg was very demanding and the workshop was stretched to satisfy his technical requirements. Although he was not interested in the technical side of printing, he did become aware of the rich possibilities of using Tyler's treasured stones. To him their surface, or 'skin' was sensual; they were 'sexy' objects to draw on and experiment with. Tyler appreciated that Rauschenberg was 'a very organised artist' and 'the consummate collaborator'.

history of collaborative printmaking. 'We kept increasing in scale', Tyler noted, 'not just because we wanted to, but the artists were actually asking for it.'

The results were fantastic. We were having some very good results with increasing the scale, because as you increase scale you also increase the other problems that are accompanying printmaking … the processes have to change, the timing and

He worked from a large collection of photographs that we would blow up to his predetermined sizes. Make either negative or positive films of these enlargements, then make photo printing plates from which we generally made a paper transfer that he would use to rub onto stones. These rubbings were usually embellished with tusche washes and crayon drawing and then the stones were processed for proofing.

(opposite) **Robert RAUSCHENBERG Banner** 1969 colour lithograph
from *Stoned Moon* series 1969–70

14

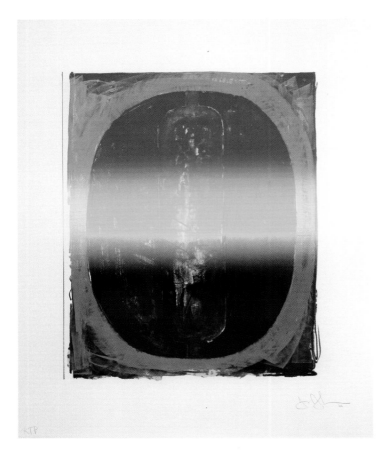

Rubylith was used to create flats and solid shapes and for masking out areas in image films during platemaking. Rauschenberg was the consummate collaborator who loved to have everyone involved for long days (often all day and all night with printers eating at the presses during our marathon proofing and drinking sessions). He liked to push the endurance equation and was very engaging, often succeeding in getting what he wanted. He loved inventing his images on the spot with only the tools and materials around him. His wit, quick eye, hand agility and ability to drink and drink and work was amazing.[17]

Rauschenberg took part in other artistic collaborations, notably in performances with composer John Cage and choreographer Merce Cunningham. The notion of 'collaboration' here was the antithesis of what took place in Tyler's studios. To avoid requiring the music to follow the dance, or the dance to follow the music, dancer and musician conceived their work as something independent of the other. The unification was the performance itself, when sets and costume, music and dance were placed within the same time frame.

'THE CRITIC SMILES'

The success of Rauschenberg's *Booster*, along with an enthusiastic and convivial sales pitch from Tyler (drawing on his experience as a travelling salesman for Thompson Wire Co.), convinced Jasper Johns that he should work with Gemini GEL. Johns arrived with a clear idea in mind. He was another who wanted to work on Tyler's 'gorgeous' stones — which had been ferreted out by Tyler from an old building site and carted away in an elderly VW with broken springs. Johns selected all the large stones and, treasuring their quality and feel, started drawing on every one of them, making a series of numerals that were printed in black, using the limestone surfaces to great advantage.

Having printed the black numerals, Johns turned his attention to printing a coloured series from the same stones as the first, but with colour rainbow rolls — the stone inked with a roller loaded with several coloured inks.

Jasper JOHNS from the *Color Numeral Series* 1969 colour lithographs
(above and opposite) **Figure 0, 1, 2, 3, 4, 5**

Printing two editions from the same stones could have been a difficult undertaking because an image can become degraded with use, so Tyler turned to a technique he had learned at Tamarind in 1963, which he had been taught by Marcel Durassier — he described it as a 'rub up technique',

a very elaborate way of capturing all the nuances of a wash that an artist applies to a stone. But it also puts [the printing surface] into slight relief. In the planographic medium of lithography, there really isn't any raised surface. It's chemical, it's flat, it is difficult to maintain, difficult to stabilise. But with Marcel's technique, with a little innovation here and there, I was able to create this very low relief that would sustain very long printings.[18]

Tyler successfully editioned the ten black numerals followed by the colour numerals, along with many proofs. The result includes lusciously coloured numbers such as *Figure 7* 1969 — with its image of a smiling *Mona Lisa*, and the artist's handprint.

Transforming the trite into beautifully wrought works of art in painting, printmaking and sculpture brought Johns to prominence during the Pop Art era. He was an admirer of the Dada artist Marcel Duchamp — whom he met through John Cage — and he drew on the Duchampian tradition of the found object. In their art, both the older man and the younger man made use of the 'ready-made', often humorous, sometimes austere.

(opposite) **Figure** 7 colour lithograph from the *Color Numeral Series* 1969
(below) Jasper Johns at Gemini GEL in 1968 with proofs from his
Black Numeral series 1968

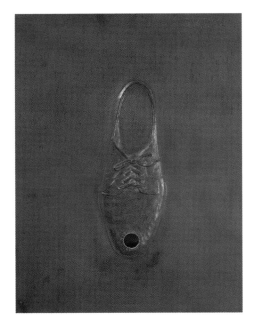  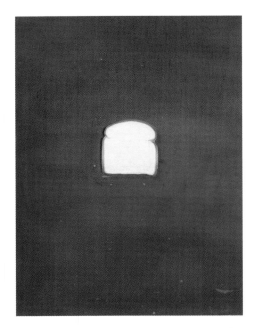

Jasper JOHNS from *Lead Reliefs* 1969
(above left to right) **High School Days** sheet lead and glass mirror relief
The Critic Smiles sheet lead, gold casting and tin leafing relief
Bread cast lead, sheet lead, paper and oil paint relief
(below) **Fragment — According to What: Leg and Chair** 1971
colour lithograph

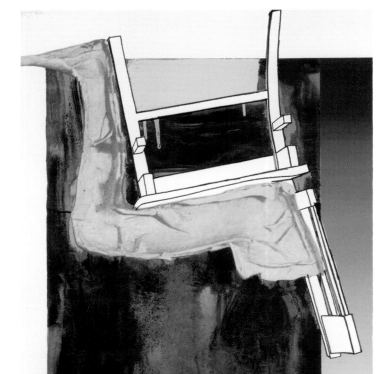

Johns appropriated and refined his own work constantly. His first *Toothbrush* of 1959 was a cast sculpmetal version of this prosaic object, with the bristles replaced by teeth.

I had the idea that in society the approval of the critic was a kind of cleansing police action. When the critic smiles it's a lopsided smile with hidden meanings. And of course a smile involves baring the teeth. The critic is keeping a certain order, which is why it is like a police function.[19]

This image of the toothbrush was to reappear, including a relief sculpture Johns made with Tyler in 1969, *The Critic Smiles*, with the image moulded in wax and plaster, then embossed into sheet lead. The teeth were cast in gold by a dentist then set on the brush, which was leafed in tin. For this 1969 series of five reliefs, including the toothbrush, Johns revisted previous subject matter, including a shoe with a mirror; a flag; a light bulb; and a slice of bread. The original intention was that these compositions should be made in the form of embossed paper, using a hydraulic Hoe platen press at the Amsco Corporation. This failed because the press tore the paper. Tyler then suggested the hardier sheet lead.[20]

The use of sculpture and sculptural techniques at Gemini GEL was a bonus for artists who worked at the workshop. At the time Johns began working at Gemini in 1969 Tyler was in the midst of his groundbreaking *Profile Airflow* project with Claes Oldenburg, and producing the

Embossed Linear Constructions of Albers. For both projects Tyler developed collaborations with mould and model makers, programmers and engraving machinists: 'I had formed a close relationship with the president of Amsco Corp (L.A.), Jim Goerz. His plant was equipped to do hot stamping on heated platen presses. He sold me one of his Hoe platen presses in 1968.' This set the scene for Johns' embossed *Alphabet* prints of 1969.

We used my engraving contact for the plate making and Amsco's San Francisco plant to emboss the papers on their large format platen press. After the success of the Black Numeral Series (June 1968 publication) and Gray Alphabets and his enjoyable collaborations with the workshop, Jasper was quite willing to continue on new projects. I was always showing the test or trial results of each project to the artists. Jasper was quick to recognize that my mould-making and press abilities for forming would be appropriate for his lead relief project. His previous experiences had been to paint plastic casts with Sculpmetal and feeble attempts to make lead reliefs in a lithography press from sheet lead passed over a relief plate. He wanted his reliefs to be sheet lead and not cast lead, which would have been very heavy. The confluence of mould and model makers, platen presses at Amsco, an interested executive Jim Goerz, and tool engineers who worked on the Airflow moulds, all made it possible for the Lead Relief Project to move ahead quickly with excellent results. By this time, Jeff Sanders, my multiple person was on board at the workshop, who was a great help managing the various component parts of the Airflow and Lead Relief projects.[21]

To ensure that the momentum of workshop practice continued, Tyler investigated new ideas to entice artists to return: 'You couldn't just keep inviting them back to make a lithograph or inviting them back to make a silk screen. You have to keep giving them something new to chew on.'[22] It wasn't sufficient to be able to offer scale; handmade paper was something Tyler also wished to offer the artists. He had completed an arist in residency at the Cranbrook Acadamy of Art, Michigan, in 1970 where he spent time working with the papermaker Lawrence Barker and his student John Koller. He believed from this experience that handmade paper offered exciting possibilities for printmaking at his workshop. He then

developed a project which originated from meetings with Vera Freeman, import paper manager, and Andrew Nelson of Whithead Paper Company, New York city, and Elie d'Humières, President of Fine Art Printing Papers, Arjomari Paper Company in Paris. They suggested that Tyler collaborate with Marius Peraudeau, who owned the thirteenth-century Richard de Bas paper mill in Ambert, France. In discussions with Peraudeau it was agreed that an American artist would go to France for an experimental project in paper. Tyler thought immediately of Rauschenberg, who was game for almost anything, extremely creative and fast on his feet. The result was a group of 12 paper works, *Pages and Fuses* of 1973–74. The *Pages* were delicately shaped works in combinations of pulp — made of natural coloured rag with additions of cords, cloth remnants and cloth tape. For *Fuses* Rauschenberg incorporated combinations of brilliantly coloured inked pulp, collaged with screenprinted tissue, to form unusual shapes such as can be seen in *Link* of 1974 — a twentieth-century version of a luminous medieval manuscript. This venture heralded the future of handmade paper in the Tyler workshops.

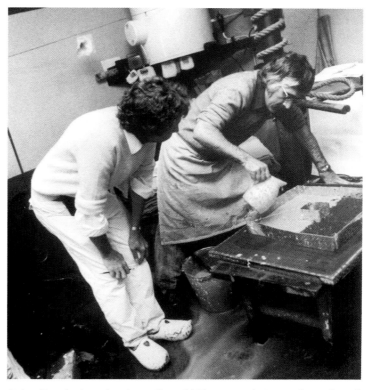

Robert Rauschenberg observing as Kenneth Tyler pours pulp into a galvanised metal image mould, which is on top of a papermaking mould, in the making of *Bit*, from the *Pages and Fuses* series, Richard de Bas paper mill, Ambert, France, August 1973 (photograph Gianfranco Gorgoni) detail

A TIME OF RE-EVALUATION

Although Gemini GEL had gained a reputation as an important print workshop with some major artistic successes, it was not necessarily appreciated widely on the east coast of America. An exhibition of prints from the workshop, *Technics and Creativity*, curated at the Museum of Modern Art by Riva Castleman in 1972, received generally negative responses. One critic for the *New York Times*, who had not actually visited the exhibition, objected to the 'catalog-object-coloring book-sales brochure' which accompanied the exhibition,

and the workshop's emphasis on artists who were 'not exactly undiscovered'.[23] More circumspect, but still critical, was Judith Goldman's article for *Print Collector's Newsletter*, noting Gemini's 'image of the Metro-Goldwyn-Mayer of lithography workshops', whose use of technologies saw it as 'the Cadillac of the expanding print and publishing industry'. She commented that 'certain artists can use Gemini's facilities, while others fail completely'.[24]

Robert **RAUSCHENBERG** **Local Means** 1970 colour lithograph
from *Stoned Moon* series 1969–70

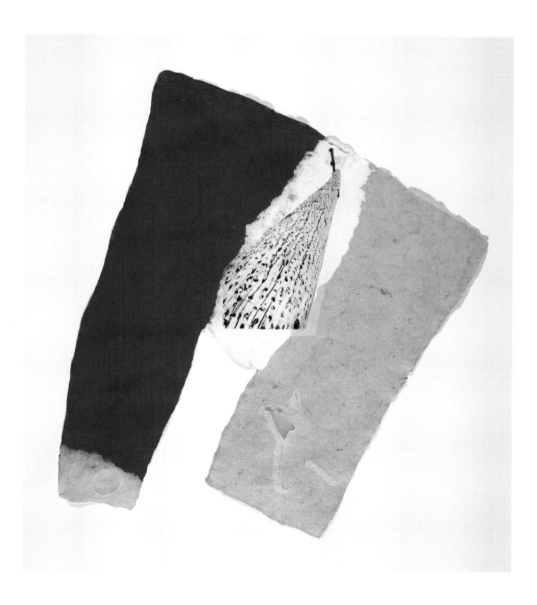

This was a time of introspection for Tyler, and ultimately he decided he would leave Gemini GEL and pursue his dream by establishing a small workshop on the east coast, near several of the artists who had worked with him in the Los Angeles workshop.

Tyler had planned to establish a workshop on Long Island, not far from the home of Roy Lichtenstein (who had worked at Gemini GEL), but environmental restrictions forced him to look elsewhere. The elsewhere was upstate New York, and the Tyler Workshop Ltd was established at Bedford in 1974, becoming Tyler Graphics Ltd at the same premises the following year, in close proximity to artists such as Anni and Josef Albers, Robert Motherwell and Frank Stella.

The inaugural project for Tyler was again with Albers, now aged in his mid-80s. It was the artist's wish to achieve something extraordinary in printmaking, and it was to screenprinting that Albers and Tyler turned, producing colour compositions with no overlap, in which all the inks were printed directly onto the white of the paper, without overprinting. Tyler used photographic techniques to expand or contract separate squares of colour on a photosensitive screen, so that each square would abut the other.[25] Such an exercise required a perfect system of registration in screenprinting, and also perfect colour matching.

Robert RAUSCHENBERG Link coloured paper pulp with collage of screenprinted tissue from the series *Pages and Fuses* 1974

Josef ALBERS
(clockwise from top left) **Gray Instrumentation II c, g, j, f** colour screenprints
from the series *Gray Instrumentation II* 1975

After a lifetime of honing his sense of colour, Albers had an extraordinary sensitivity to its subtleties. He demanded and received perfect colour matching, which was essential for the success of this and other print projects. The artist would bring a leaf or a twig and ask Tyler to replicate the colour exactly in ink. After making many proofs in the new intimate premises, with a small staff, their first joint effort in screenprinting at Bedford Village was *Gray Instrumentation I* in 1974 and *Gray Instrumentation II* the following year (two of four portfolios). Such precision in screenprinting had not been seen before. With Tyler, Albers produced these remarkable works shortly before he died in 1976.

Notes

1. Neil Welliver, 'Albers on Albers', *ARTnews*, 64(9) January 1966, p. 48.
2. Brenda Danilowitz, *The Prints of Josef Albers: a catalogue raisonné 1915–1976*, New York: Hudson Hills Press, in association with the Josef and Anni Albers Foundation, 2001, cat. nos 157 and 158, pp. 97–101.
3. According to Albers, 'Color deceives continually … the same color evokes innumerable readings. Instead of mechanically applying or merely implying laws and rules of color harmony, distinct color effects are produced — through recognition of the interaction of color', in Josef Albers, *Interaction of Color*, New Haven, London: Yale University Press, 1975, p. 1.
4. *Josef Albers: White Line Squares* (exhibition catalogue), Los Angeles: Los Angeles County Museum of Art and Gemini GEL, 1966, p. 19, cited in Brenda Danilowitz, *The Prints of Josef Albers: a catalogue raisonné 1915–1976*, New York: Hudson Hills Press, in association with the Josef and Anni Albers Foundation, 2001, p. 27.
5. Pat Gilmour, *Ken Tyler, Master Printer, and the American Print Renaissance*, Canberra: National Gallery of Australia, 1986, p. 39.
6. Ken Tyler, transcript of undated telephone call with Josef Albers, 1966, copy held by Jane Kinsman.
7. Fernand Mourlot, *Gravés dans ma mémoire: cinquante ans de lithographie avec Picasso, Matisse, Chagall, Braque, Miró …*, Paris: Editions Robert Laffont, 1979, pp. 99–100.
8. Ken Tyler, correspondence with Jane Kinsman, 25 July 2002.
9. Ken Tyler, in *Reaching Out: Ken Tyler, master printer* (documentary film), Avery Tirce Productions, 1976.
10. Interview with John Stix, Black Mountain College Project Papers, North Carolina State Archives, Raleigh, no 179, 8 May 1972, quoted in May Emma Harris, 'Josef Albers: art education at Black Mountain College', in *Josef Albers: a retrospective* (exhibition catalogue), New York: Solomon R. Guggenheim Museum, 1988, p. 55.
11. Mary Lynn Kotz, *Rauschenberg: art and life*, New York: Harry N. Abrams, 1990, p. 66.
12. Ken Tyler, correspondence with Jane Kinsman, 21 June 2002. Tyler continues, 'It's interesting for me to now reflect on whom I was trying to work with in January and February of 1966. I visited Mark Rothko, Hans Hofmann, Edward Hopper and Ben Shahn in January. The same month I talked with Andrew Wyeth, Larry Rivers, Bill de Kooning and Mark Tobey, who I visited in February.'
13. Ken Tyler, correspondence with Jane Kinsman, 17 June 2002. Rauschenberg had used the body as early as 1949 in his *Blueprint* series.
14. Ronny Cohen, 'The Medium Isn't the Message', *ARTnews*, 84(8) October 1985, p. 76.
15. Robert Rauschenberg, 'Notes on Stoned Moon', *Studio International* 178(917), November 1969, 178, pp. 247–250.
16. Ken Tyler, Qantas Birthday Lecture, 14 October 1999, National Gallery of Australia, Canberra.
17. Ken Tyler, correspondence with Jane Kinsman, 11 June 2002.
18. Ken Tyler, Qantas Birthday Lecture, 14 October 1999, National Gallery of Australia, Canberra.
19. Michael Crichton, *Jasper Johns*, New York: Harry N. Abrams and the Whitney Museum of Art, 1977, p. 42.
20. Penelope Edmonds and Martha Simpson, 'Collaboration in the conservation of Jasper Johns' lead reliefs', unpublished manuscript, copy held by Jane Kinsman.
21. Ken Tyler, correspondence with Jane Kinsman, 21 June 2002.
22. Ken Tyler, Qantas Birthday Lecture, 14 October 1999, National Gallery of Australia, Canberra.
23. Hilton Kramer, '"Technics" of Fashion', *New York Times*, 2 May 1971, section 2, p. 21.
24. Judith Goldman, 'Gemini Prints at the Museum of Modern Art', *Print Collector's Newsletter*, 2(2) May–June 1971, p. 30.
25. See Donald Karshan, 'One to One: Ken Tyler with Donald Karshan', *The Artist and the Master Printer: innovation by collaboration* (exhibition catalogue), Daytona Beach, Florida: Daytona Beach Community College, 1989, p. 12, for the use of photography at Tyler's workshop.

Typewriter Pointillism
Roy Lichtenstein

Roy Lichtenstein worked with Ken Tyler at both his west and east coast workshops, beginning at Gemini GEL in 1969. Many of the projects they embarked on together were fuelled by the artist's inquisitiveness. What happens when blue is used instead of yellow? What happens when an image in one medium is transposed into another? The apparently mechanical style of Lichstentein's art was not so much a product of the techniques employed, it was the look, the aesthetic the artist desired.

Before the Second World War Lichtenstein had made 'some appalling paintings … a kind of Reginald Marsh [Social] realism'.[1] He was drafted for the war effort in February 1943 and from February 1945 served in the European theatre in England, France, Belgium and Germany. While still in the army, the young soldier came to the attention of an officer, Irv Novick, who shared an interest in art. Novick went on to become a cartoonist for DC Comics, whose publications, such as *All-American Men of War* and *GI Combat*, became inspirational source material for Lichtenstein — his fighter pilot compositions of the 1960s, for example.[2] This imagery reappeared in the *Reflections* series Lichtenstein made towards the end of his life, published by Tyler Graphics.

After his demobilisation in January 1946, Lichtenstein returned to the study of fine art at Ohio State University — a course he had begun before his wartime experiences. He received financial support under legislation that became known as the GI Bill, which provided education and training for returned service personnel. He completed postgraduate studies and worked as an instructor at Ohio, while evolving a European-inspired style of semi-abstraction. Later, in 1957, he dabbled in an Abstract Expressionist style before he embraced Pop Art, becoming a key American figure in that movement.

Lichtenstein developed an original aesthetic during the early 1960s that paradoxically highlighted industrial printing methods derived from his sources of inspiration. He adopted the subject matter of popular culture, of action movies and comics, romantic potboilers, advertisements, manufactured objects and items of food, such as in his paintings *Kitchen Stove* of 1961–62 and *Peanut Butter Cup* of 1962. These were rendered to achieve a mechanical look using the Ben Day dot system — a commercial printing technique used to denote halftones, named after the American illustrator Benjamin Day. On the side of the stove, for example, the eye mixes the colour of the dots (blue) and the colour of the background (white), which gives the appearance of a lighter blue. Lichtenstein's marriage of commercial subject matter with a masterful technique produced a double-edged art characterised by a keen wit and a sardonic style.

Roy LICHTENSTEIN
(opposite) **Kitchen Stove** 1961–62 oil on canvas
(right) **Brushstroke** 1967 colour screenprint

THE FUNNIES

From the early to mid-60s, Lichtenstein began to make a name for himself as an artist, albeit rather notoriously, particularly with his exhibitions at the Leo Castelli Gallery in New York. From 1962 to 1967, colour lithographic and screenprinted posters, such as his war comic inspired *Crak!* of 1963–64 or *Brushstroke* of 1967 — his Pop take on Abstract Expressionism — were issued at the time of each exhibition.

The reaction to Lichtenstein's first showing at the Castelli Gallery during February and March 1962 ranged from open hostility and incomprehension to bemused misunderstanding, coupled with an appreciation of the formal properties of his art. Writing for *ARTnews*, Natalie Edgar complained that Lichtenstein 'disappoints our expectations that an absurd iconography would produce humor'.

Why shouldn't the comic strips be funny in 'serious' painting? … Certainly they proclaim their intent to be ugly for they are careful blow-ups of their newspaper prototypes — lithography dots, mechanical hatching, acidic color and primitive drawing and macrocephalic heads and BLAM (a direct hit on a plane) are all carefully reproduced … One could expect that a grotesque thing that had a comic content in itself would be doubly humorous. But we are doubly disappointed … It is not transformed by esthetics, it replaces esthetics. So what was grotesque in the funnies, stays grotesque in its replacement — only doubly so.[3]

Less critical, but also lacking an understanding of Lichtenstein's work, was the artist Donald Judd.

Roy LICHTENSTEIN
(above) **Crak!** 1963–64 colour lithograph
(opposite) **Shipboard Girl** 1965 colour lithograph

This time he was described in the *New York Times* as 'One of the worst artists in America', who, using a method of 'typewriter pointillism . . .[made] a sow's ear out of a sow's ear'.[5] Such outrage inspired a *Life* magazine article of 31 January 1964 entitled 'Is he the worst artist in the US?' Clearly, the adoption of comic strip subject matter offended.

The extraordinary talent of this artist has come to be fully appreciated. Tyler recently credited Lichtenstein with making many beautiful prints that helped keep the print revival alive.

From his early prints (late 40s and 50s) Roy demonstrates a love for graphic expression. Looking at the hundreds of prints, posters, and multiples he made, I think one has to say he was one of the most successful printmakers of his generation. His prints were always well crafted and used many times the newest print technology to give them a cutting edge look.[6]

HEARTFELT

Lichtenstein developed his Pop Art in several steps after flirting with Abstract Expressionism, as did many of his generation. Yet even at that early stage in his development, he would paint into his works hidden comic images from the repertoire of Disney characters, such as Donald Duck, Bugs Bunny and Mickey Mouse —seen by the artist as 'an anti art symbol'. During this time he made little drawings after bubble-gum wrappers for his sons David Hoyt and Mitchell Wilson Lichtenstein. This popular commercial imagery inspired the artist: 'It occurred to me to do one of these bubble gum wrappers, as is, large, just to see what it would look like.'[7]

Turning to other popular imagery such as comic and romance strips, and to avoid the often muddy look found in these cheap printings, Lichtenstein purified his palette, focusing on primary colours and black and white. The dull colouring of his original source material — strips such as girls' romances, *Falling in Love*, *Girls' Love Stories*, *Young Romance* and *Secret Hearts*, drawn by the likes of Tony Abruzzo — became lighter and bolder. He also subtly altered the compositions,

Judd's criticism, published in *Arts Magazine,* was that the adoption of the imagery from comic strips could be used in the context of some social comment; but Lichtenstein was not doing that, therefore the art fell short of the mark.

The funny papers have again caused outrage among the respectable; this time it is not morals but art that is being corrupted … Lichtenstein's comics and advertisements destroy the necessity to which the usual definitions pretend … It is not so unusual to appreciate the directness of comics; they looked like Léger, as do these versions of them.

Likening the 'commercial' look to that of Léger, but 'hardly as good', Judd nevertheless admired the formal properties of Lichtenstein's art: 'He has added slightly to the ways of being open and raw. Ironically, the composition is expert, and some of it is quite traditional.'[4] The hostility continued with Lichtenstein's next show at the Castelli Gallery in September and October 1963.

carefully recomposing the imagery, often by cropping, simplifying and enlarging, producing something more refined, with a flat, patterned quality.

Lichtenstein came to appreciate the fact that the more seemingly detached the subject, or the more deadpan, then paradoxically the more evocative his art became.

At the beginning I wasn't sure exactly what I was doing, but I was very excited about, and interested in, the highly emotional content yet detached, impersonal handling of love, hate, war, etc, in these cartoon images … The closer my work is to the original, the more threatening and critical the content. However, my work is entirely transformed in that my purpose and perception are entirely different. I think my paintings are critically transformed.[8]

By the mid-1960s, his work was revealing a tension and sensibility produced by a combination of the deadpan industrial look with heartfelt emotion or life and death experiences. An example is his 1964 painting *Kiss V,* derived from a preliminary drawing made the year before.

I was more strictly imitating industrial printing. Now the dots have become something else … more brutal, more antiseptic, and more present-day.[9]

In his art Lichtenstein enhanced the look of cheap printings. He would work with the lightest colour first, stencilling the dots and completing the composition with the black outline — which originated in commercial printing, where it covered a multitude of missed colour registrations.

INDUSTRIAL IMPRESSIONISM

Lichtenstein went on to make prints of great beauty. He drew his imagery not only from popular culture of one kind or another, but in some instances from art history. Along with subjects from comic books, he turned to landscapes, or moonscapes, seascapes and sunrises. In the later years of the 1960s, he became interested in Claude Monet. His fascination with the French Impressionist's paintings developed following discussions with John Coplans, who was curating an exhibition for the Pasadena Art Museum, *Serial Imagery*, which opened in

September 1968. Coplans provided Lichtenstein with photographs of Monet's works that were included in the exhibition catalogue. These formed the basis of Lichtenstein's series of paintings and prints of haystacks and Rouen cathedral. Tyler described the process:

Roy used punched 'dot stencils' in his New York City studio for making his paintings. The stencils were cut out to his drawn shapes, pasted onto the canvas and acrylic paint was applied through the stencil dots to the canvas. [For the prints] we used the same 'dot stencils', exposed them to a photo sensitive plate to produce a positive printing dot. The Haystack and Cathedral images were cut in Rubylith from Roy Lichtenstein's original ink drawings. These Rubyliths were used to mask off areas in the all over dot films to create the printing images.[10]

The Monet prints of 1969 were the first works Lichtenstein made at Gemini GEL. The artist saw the great opportunities of working there: 'There are very few places where you can make a mark and have 15 people work on it.'[11] Gemini and Lichtenstein were made for each other. The artist's 'machine' aesthetic was particularly suited to the workshop's methods, and to the look of Gemini publications. Ironically, however, such a look required the application of immense effort and skill by Tyler and the workshop team to achieve purity of line, unsullied colour and accurate registration

Lichtenstein usually came to the workshop very well prepared for a particular project, as well as for the social interaction that the occasion provided. 'He was a marvellous person to be around', Tyler recalled. Along with a new set of jokes, stories and music for the team, Lichtenstein brought his plans for the work.

Roy always worked from 1) a sketch; 2) finished drawing or 3) collage as his preparatory material for making a print or multiple. To correct the first trial proofs he often used collage with notations … Roy avoided making color proofs and resisted color changes during proofing because his preparatory material was his guide. Pushing the dimension of printmaking was not his purpose in making prints.[12]

The *Cathedral* and *Haystack* series, groups of eight and ten prints, were begun and completed in 1969. Unlike Lichtenstein's Monet paintings, every one a different image, each print series is derived from one single image. He used brilliant primary colours, coupled with black and white in different combinations, to create the impression of various times of the day, together with his signature method of incorporating Ben Day dots for tonal values.

On one level, the *Cathedral* and *Haystack* prints can be interpreted as following Monet's exploration of light and the passage of time. In Lichtenstein's words, they are 'supposed to be times of day'; which he qualified by adding: 'only because that is the way *his* were, and because it's kind of silly and fortuitous and obviously not about daylight at all'.[13] On some of the prints being in a single colour, Lichtenstein explained: 'I like to represent the complexities of impressionism in one color.' Asked which image represented morning, he replied:

I guess yellow. It's all a pretty abstract idea ... the purplish ones in red and blue are evening ... The black is on a flat blue color; that's midnight, it's most invisible ... Red and yellow stands for daylight.[14]

The prints are also about looking. The combinations of colours, the motif and the dot screens provide for a range of viewing effects. The motif may appear to dissolve before the viewer's eyes, aided by the fact that, unlike so many of Lichtenstein's cartoon-inspired images, his Monet series of prints lacks the heavy outline in black used to define previous subjects.

For the *Haystack* series, lithography was augmented by screenprinting to obtain a brilliant white, unachievable through the use of lithography alone. The Tyler workshop's use of a whole spectrum of printing methods, which began while Rauschenberg and Johns worked at Gemini GEL, continued to evolve with collaborations with Lichtenstein.

Lichtenstein enjoyed experimenting and investigating new ideas while making images in print. After completing the *Haystack* and *Cathedral* paintings and the print series,

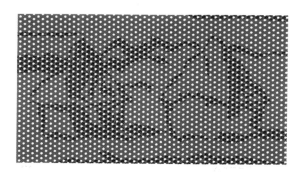

Roy LICHTENSTEIN
(from top) **Haystack #1** 1969 colour lithograph, screenprint
Haystack #5 1969 colour lithograph, screenprint
Haystack #6, State I 1969 colour lithograph

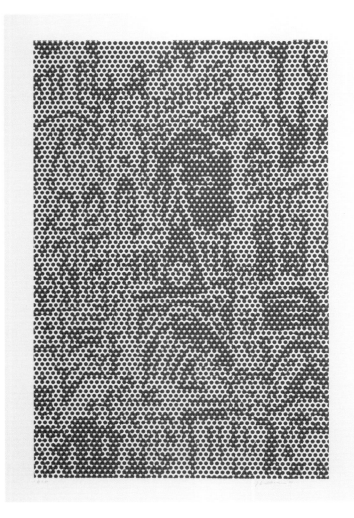

he concluded that the actual printing process enhanced his work. He compared the two exercises.

In terms of exactness of placement and register, the prints are better ... because they can be better controlled in this medium. Working on canvas isn't controllable in the same way. The paintings bear the tracks of corrections of various things. The prints are all worked out beforehand and appear purer.[15]

The paintings of Rouen cathedral celebrate commercial printing techniques — in the words of the artist, they are 'paintings about printing', while the prints are 'in the style of cheap printings brought back again to

Roy LICHTENSTEIN
(above left to right) **Cathedral #4** 1969 colour lithograph
Cathedral #6, State I 1969 colour lithograph

printings — elegant printings'.[16] The pristine nature of these Monet prints with a mass production look resulted in the creative tension between the evocation of the original beauty of the Monets, the commercial look of the artist's unique style and the exquisite nature of the Gemini GEL printings — what Lichtenstein called an 'industrial impressionism'.

ARTE MODERNE

If one of Lichtenstein's art historical references was Monet, the early twentieth-century art styles of Expressionism, Cubism and Art Deco were also sources of inspiration — but it was the appearance not the theory that was important to him. 'I don't dwell on the differences in viewing space in art history. For example, I can see the obvious difference between Renaissance and

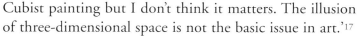

Cubist painting but I don't think it matters. The illusion of three-dimensional space is not the basic issue in art.'[17]

In 1968, while in Los Angeles, Lichtenstein had seen a group of portrait heads by Alexei von Jawlensky in the Pasadena Art Museum. These inspired the *Modern Head* series of 1970. 'What in the world a modern head could be about', interested him.

I mean to make a man look like a machine. It's the machine quality of the twenties and thirties that interests me. Picasso and Braque in Analytical Cubism weren't particularly interested in the machine aspect. It got consciously much more that way in Léger's painting and with the Futurists and Constructivists, the people portrayed becoming dehumanized by being related to machines. This relates strongly to comic book images, which are not machine-like but are largely the product of machine thinking … The art moderne idea of making a head into something that looks as if it's been made by an engineering draftsman deals with industrialization and manufacture, which is what my painting has dealt with since '61 or so.[18]

Lichtenstein's take on modernist heads can be seen in a group of five prints and one relief. *Modern Head #5*, for example, depicts a 'dehumanised' head in profile in a colour lithograph on an engraved and anodised aluminium support. To achieve the desired perfectly finished high-tech look, Tyler approached Angell Manufacturing to create the plates, which were then printed on a special automatic flat-bed press.

Lichtenstein's next print series, made with Tyler in 1970, was *Peace Through Chemistry*, a group of five prints using lithography and screenprinting — sometimes in concert, sometimes separately — and one relief. The artist described the imagery as 'muralesque' — 'they are a little like WPA murals'.[19] Each composition consists of a head in profile, with chemistry paraphernalia and a machine-like, Art Deco look.

Roy LICHTENSTEIN
(above left to right) **Modern Head #4** 1970 colour lithograph, engraving on anodised aluminium
Modern Head #5 1970 embossed graphite with Strathmore die-cut paper overlay on anodised aluminium

33

All the works relate to earlier iconography of the mid-to late sixties, such as that seen in his 1965 Castelli poster *This Must be The Place*, or his poster for the film festival at the Lincoln Center the following year. The poster had a similar thirties look.[20] These works were stepping stones that took the artist towards *Peace Through Chemistry*.

To round out the exploration of arte moderne, two sculptures, the brass *Untitled Head I* and *Untitled Head II* in walnut — were also made at Gemini GEL, taking their cue from the earlier modernist series.

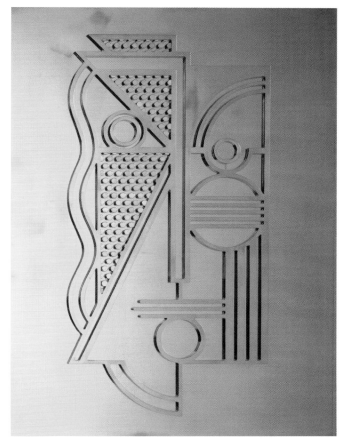

Roy LICHTENSTEIN
(opposite top) **Peace Through Chemistry I** 1970 colour lithograph, screenprint
(opposite below left to right) **Untitled Head I** 1970 brass
Untitled Head II 1970 California English walnut
(above) **Peace Through Chemistry Bronze** 1970 cast bronze relief
(right) **Modern Head Relief** 1970 brass

MULTIPLE TECHNIQUES

In subsequent years of working with Tyler, Lichtenstein liked to investigate the possibilities of combining techniques, such as the lithography, silkscreening and linecut used in the *Bull Profile* series of 1973. He found printmaking useful for the progression of his art because he could amend and edit it during the proofing stage: 'you print certain things, and then work on the print, and maybe we go further'. For example, beginning with a lithograph based on a collage, he would then

work on top of that thing and change it some more. But I think that's what's interesting about printing, is that you can try another colour on the same shape. It's a fairly simple thing to do. And it's all that kind of very quick changes that you can do, you can see it immediately in a variety of colours and prints in different ways.[21]

Lichtenstein's experimentation with style was particularly evident in the *Bull Profile* series. Citing his sources of inspiration for these works as a Picasso bull and Van Doesburg's cows, Lichtenstein enjoyed the way he could progressively work the subject out as he moved towards greater abstraction.

I didn't want to destroy the bull in doing it, you know, because whatever else I was doing, it had to look like a bull. I mean, all of the marks that are made are made for other reasons, but it can't look unlike a bull, it would be inconsistent with the idea ... It is really more that I'm doing this from the preceding one. It's like taking the theme of the one in front of it, and using it and changing it a bit, and making it less realistic.[22]

Roy LICHTENSTEIN
(from top) **Bull I** 1973 linecut
Bull II 1973 colour lithograph, linecut
Bull VII 1973 colour lithograph, screenprint, linecut

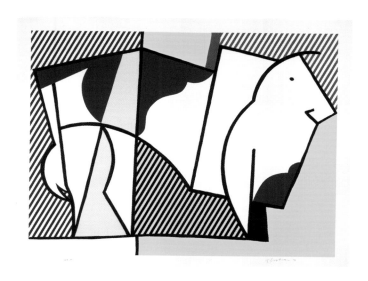

Roy LICHTENSTEIN
(from top left) **Bull III** 1973 colour lithograph, screenprint, linecut
Bull IV 1973 colour lithograph, screenprint, linecut
Bull V 1973 colour lithograph, screenprint, linecut

The next prints produced with Tyler were made at the new east coast workshop in Bedford Village, upstate New York. In 1976 Lichtenstein completed the complex and innovative series of *Entablatures*. Consisting of 11 prints, the series combined screenprinting, lithography, embossing and collage to produce a remarkable three-dimensional quality. The works derived from a sequence of *Frieze* paintings that Lichtenstein had completed earlier in the 1970s, which were based on photographs the artist took in New York of nineteenth-century neoclassical buildings.

Research for this print series began in 1974, and it progressed by trial and error. Working with collage, embossing and foil, Tyler started experimenting. Using deeply embossed dies and cast bronze plates as the technical solution to the problem of creating a sense of the third dimension, Tyler looked outside the workshop and to various east coast and west coast engineering firms. In the end, he had the required metal dies machined at Drake Engineering, in Danbury, Connecticut, the plates

Roy LICHTENSTEIN
(below) **Entablature III** 1976 colour screenprint, lithography, metal foil collage, embossing
(far below) **Entablature II** 1976 colour screenprint, lithograph, metal foil collage, embossing

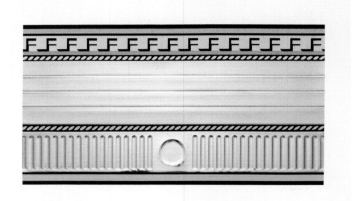

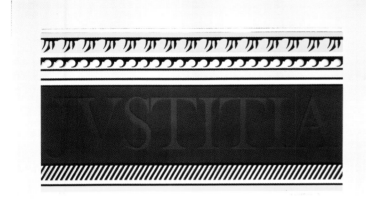

processed at Swan Engraving, in Bridgeport, Connecticut, the bronze cast at Tallix Foundry, in Beacon, New York, and the machining of the metal dies done at Tomkins Tooling, in Gardena, California. The resulting plates, from which the *Entablatures* were printed, are now housed at the National Gallery of Australia. The editioning of such complicated prints was a nightmare — sometimes the workshop could complete the edition run of 30; at other times only 16 were achieved.

Aside from its extraordinary technical innovation, the *Entablatures* series reveals a fanciful range of intricate ornamental forms such as meanders, rosettes, scrolls and spirals in elegant colour combinations, with the Latin word 'Justitia' included on two of the works. Riva Castleman of the Museum of Modern Art, New York, described Lichtenstein's involvement in the workshop as a hands-off approach, allowing the workshop freedom to innovate in such a complex exercise to achieve the design and look the artist required.

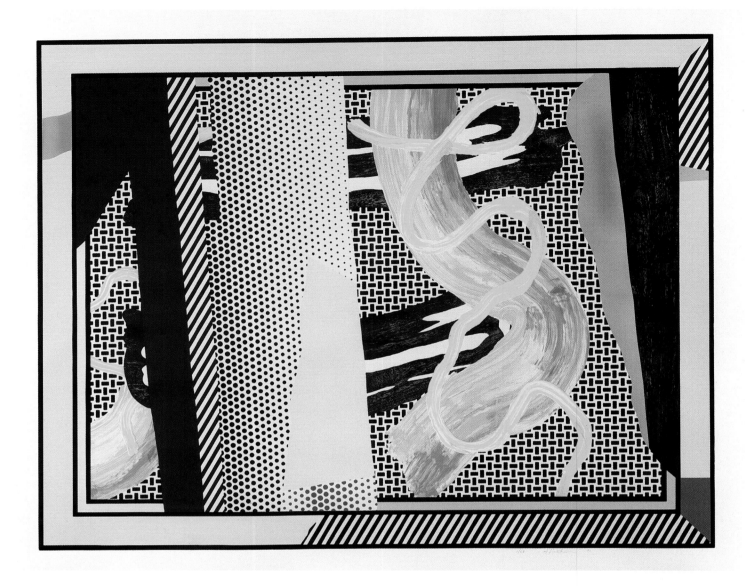

REFLECTIONS

The next time Lichtenstein and Tyler would attempt something as technically complex as the *Entablatures* was in 1989 when they began the *Reflections* series. This group of seven works is an outstanding exercise in printmaking: the workshop used lithography, screenprinting, relief printing with a metallised PVC collage and embossing.

The project was carried out in the new premises at Mount Kisco (opened in January 1987), where all the technical requirements could be provided in house. For Tyler it was like offering artists 'candy at the candy store'; whatever the artist desired with whatever technique they needed, 'We could pull it off. We had all the machinery to do it.'[23.] The *Reflections* prints were so large and complex that the various processes were pushed to the very limit, while demanding that the printer achieve perfect registration and keep the paper, with all its collage and embossing, intact. The series was important for the development of Lichtenstein's subject matter, for it showed the artist contemplating what he once considered the anti-contemplative nature of his early work.

One such *Reflection* is of a brushstroke. In the mid-1960s, Lichtenstein had begun a group of brushstroke paintings. 'I had played on the idea before', he recalled 'it started with a comic book image of a mad artist crossing out, with a large brushstroke "X".'[24] Lichtenstein turned to concentrate on the brushstroke itself.

Roy LICHTENSTEIN Reflections on Brushstrokes 1990 colour lithograph, screenprint, woodcut, metalised PVC plastic film collage, embossing

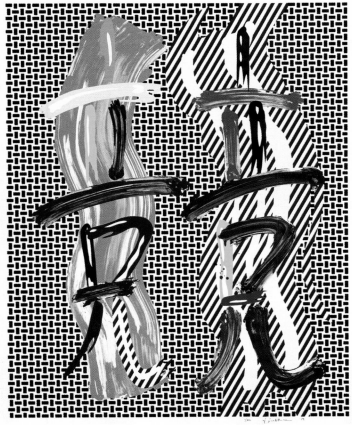

I was very interested in characterizing or caricaturing a brushstroke. The very nature of a brushstroke is anathema to outlining and filling in as used in cartoons. So I developed a form for it, which is what I am trying to do in the explosions, airplanes, and people — that is, to get a standardized thing — a stamp or image ... I got the idea very early because of the Mondrian and Picasso paintings, which inevitably led to the idea of a de Kooning. The brushstrokes obviously refer to Abstract Expressionism.[25]

Producing a lively gestural form graphically proved complex and difficult.

I had trouble with the Brush-strokes too: they looked like slices of bacon or something, they didn't really look anything like brush-strokes when I started. And I got this idea that I would use India ink on acetate and make a brush-stroke, and it made a very interesting brush stroke, because the acetate kind of repels the ink. And then I would copy. I would draw pictures of those and it was just a way of getting an idea for a brush-stroke. It had more interest than I could get by trying to dream one up.[26]

Lichtenstein returned to the brushstroke theme again and again. It had appeared in the screenprinted poster published by Leo Castelli in 1967, which became the motif for the Lichtenstein retrospective exhibition curated by John Coplans for the Pasadena Art Museum in 1968. This exhibition then travelled to the Walker Art Museum, Minneapolis, and the Stedelijk Museum, Amsterdam. The subject reappeared in many guises in the 1980s, in painting and print series of landscapes and seascapes and in anthropomorphic forms. Exploring the tension between the fluid nature of the motif and the essentially static nature of the medium, Lichtenstein produced witty brushstroke sculptures at Tyler Graphics, such as *Brushstroke VI* of 1986. A comparable tension appears in the prints *Brushstroke on Canvas* and *Brushstroke Contest* both of 1989, where the robust gestural forms are at complete odds with the static forms of the stylised canvas.

Roy LICHTENSTEIN
(from top) **Brushstroke on Canvas** 1989 colour lithograph
Brushstroke Contest 1989 colour lithograph

Other themes in the *Reflections* series also draw on the subjects first seen in Lichtenstein's work of the 1960s, the fighter pilots and blonde beauties. Made decades later, the *Reflections* reinterpret and refine the earlier paintings and prints drawn from cartoons, romance and war comics or from other artists' work. In *Reflections on Crash* 1990, for example, we see the Indian–American pilot, Johnny Cloud — the mystical, super-cool hero, derived from Irv Novick's *All-American Men of War* comic series — glancing sideways in response to the loud explosion of enemy fire, denoted by the words 'CRASH'. In Lichtenstein's re-examination of the art of the past in *Reflections on The Scream*, we see the cartoon character of baby Swee'-pea — the offspring of Popeye and Olive Oyl — whose howling face refers to the Expressionist painting *Scream* by Edvard Munch.

Roy LICHTENSTEIN
(above) **Reflections on Crash** 1990 colour lithograph, screenprint, woodcut, metalised PVC plastic film collage, embossing
(opposite above) **Reflections on The Scream** 1990 colour lithograph, screenprint, woodcut, metalised PVC plastic film collage, embossing
(opposite below left to right) **Reflections on Girl** 1990 colour lithograph, screenprint, woodcut, metalised PVC plastic film collage, embossing
Reflections on Minerva 1990 colour lithograph, screenprint, woodcut, metalised PVC plastic film collage, embossing

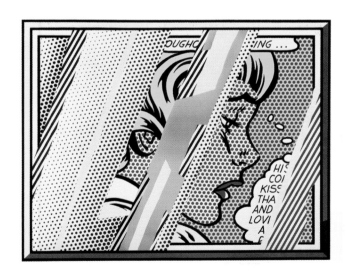

NUDES

When making relief prints, Lichtenstein would always insist on carving the wood himself. He liked the resistance of the material and having the ability to achieve the line he wanted. Paradoxically, at the proofing stage, the artist wanted to rid himself of the grainy look of the works. In *Nudes*, he adopted a new method of relief printing. For this last series Lichtenstein made at Tyler Graphics before his death in 1997, he agreed to make these works using an innovative method of printing from plastic relief plates, which Tyler had proposed.

By the time we started to work on the Nudes series in 1993 I had already engaged Bob Swan of Swan Engraving at Roy's request to make very true dot stencils for use in his studio. The thin paper was like a release paper so ink did not absorb into the surface during the painting of the dots onto the canvas. We used the dot stencils master films by Swan to create the dot plate positive films for the Nudes series. The positive key black line drawings were cut in Rubylith by Roy. He made original collages for each print from our printed color dots and solid colors. These were our maquettes for making dot shapes and solid shapes. All printing plates were photo plastic Toray printing plates.[27]

For *Nude with Yellow Pillow*, *Nude with Blue Hair* and *Roommates* of 1994, Lichtenstein reinterpreted the type of comic strip imagery he first used in the 1960s. In this last collaboration with Tyler, it appeared that Lichtenstein had turned full circle. But his treatment of the old subject matter was radically different. In these later works, for example, he made an interesting addition to the compositions — chiaroscuro. 'With my nudes', Lichtenstein remarked,

I wanted to mix artistic conventions that you would think are incompatible, namely chiaroscuro and local color, and see what happened. I'd seen something similar in Léger's work. My nudes are part light and shade, and so are the backgrounds, with dots to indicate the shade. The dots are also graduated from large to small, which usually suggests modeling in people's minds, but that's not what you get with these figures. I don't really know why I chose nudes. I'd never done them before, so that maybe something, but I also felt chiaroscuro would look good

on a body. And with my nudes there's so little sense of body flesh or skin tones — they're so unrealistic — that using them underscored the separation between reality and artistic convention.[28]

The *Nudes*, like the series *Reflections*, are key examples of Lichtenstein's late Pop Art style, which emerged in the 1990s. This style was one of great complexity and refinement, but one which also alluded to his past. Although he returned to the imagery in his scrapbooks of teen romances and war comics, he transformed it. The bathing beauties who populated the DC comic books are now nude and set in pastiches of earlier iconography — the everyday objects, the interiors and scenes drawn from advertisements. The artist executed these compositions in a lightened palette and with his ever-present sardonic wit.

Roy LICHTENSTEIN
(above) **Nude with Yellow Pillow** 1994 colour relief print
(opposite) **Nude with Blue Hair** 1994 colour relief print

44

Roy LICHTENSTEIN Roommates 1994 colour relief print

Roy Lichtenstein, February 1989 (photograph Marabeth Cohen-Tyler)

Notes

1. Roy Lichtenstein, quoted in Michael Kimmelman, *Portraits: talking with artists at the Met, the Modern, the Louvre and elsewhere*, New York: the Modern Library, 1999, p. 84.
2. See chapter 'Comics' in Kirk Varnedoe and Adam Gopnik, *Hi & Lo: modern art and popular culture*, New York: Museum of Modern Art, 1990, especially pp. 194–208.
3. Natalie Edgar, 'Reviews and Previews', *ARTNews*, 61(1) March 1962, p. 14.
4. Donald Judd, 'In the Galleries', *Arts Magazine*, 36(7) April 1962, pp. 52–53.
5. Brian O'Doherty, 'Lichtenstein: doubtful but definite triumph of the banal', *New York Times*, 27 October 1963.
6. Ken Tyler, correspondence with Jane Kinsman, 1 August 2002.
7. Bruce Glaser, 'Oldenburg, Lichtenstein, Warhol: a discussion', in John Coplans (ed.), *Roy Lichtenstein*, London: Allen Lane, the Penguin Press, 1973, p. 56.
8. John Coplans, 'An Interview with Roy Lichtenstein', in John Coplans (ed.), *Roy Lichtenstein*, London: Allen Lane, the Penguin Press, 1973, p. 52.
9. Alan Solomon, 'Conversation with Lichtenstein', in John Coplans (ed.), *Roy Lichtenstein*, London: Allen Lane, the Penguin Press, 1973, p. 85.
10. Ken Tyler, correspondence with Jane Kinsman, 11 June 2002. Rubylith is a red film used in screenprinting as a stencil that adheres to the screen.
11. Roy Lichtenstein, in Joseph E. Young, 'Lichtenstein: printmaker', *Art and Artists*, 10, March 1970, quoted in Ruth E. Fine, 'Dots, Stripes, Strokes and Foils: Roy Lichtenstein's high-tech classicism', in Mary Lee Corlett, *The Prints of Roy Lichtenstein: a catalogue raisonné 1948–1993*, New York: Hudson Hills Press in association with the National Gallery of Art, Washington, 1994, p. 30.
12. Ken Tyler, correspondence with Jane Kinsman, 29 May 2002.
13. Frederic Tuten, 'Lichtenstein at Gemini', in John Coplans (ed.), *Roy Lichtenstein*, London: Allen Lane, the Penguin Press, 1973, p. 99.
14. John Coplans, 'Interview: Roy Lichtenstein', in John Coplans (ed.), *Roy Lichtenstein*, London: Allen Lane, the Penguin Press, 1973, p. 104.
15. Roy Lichtenstein, quoted in Mary Lee Corlett, *The Prints of Roy Lichtenstein: a catalogue raisonné 1948–1993*, New York: Hudson Hills Press in association with the National Gallery of Art, Washington, 1994, p. 96.
16. Roy Lichtenstein, quoted in Frederic Tuten, 'Lichtenstein at Gemini', in John Coplans (ed.), *Roy Lichtenstein*, London: Allen Lane, the Penguin Press, 1973, pp. 98–99, quoted in Mary Lee Corlett, *The Prints of Roy Lichtenstein: a catalogue raisonné 1948–1993*, New York: Hudson Hills Press in association with the National Gallery of Art, Washington, 1994, p. 96.
17. Bruce Glaser, 'Oldenburg, Lichtenstein, Warhol: a discussion', *Artforum*, 4(6) February 1966, p. 22.
18. Roy Lichtenstein, quoted in Mary Lee Corlett, *The Prints of Roy Lichtenstein: a catalogue raisonné 1948–1993*, New York: Hudson Hills Press in association with the National Gallery of Art, Washington, 1994, p. 111.
19. John Coplans, 'Interview: Roy Lichtenstein', in John Coplans (ed.), *Roy Lichtenstein*, London: Allen Lane, the Penguin Press, 1973, p. 99; the WPA was the Works Progress Administration, later to be known as the Works Projects Administration. This was established in 1933 and employed artists on various cultural programs, until it concluded in 1943.
20. Mary Lee Corlett, *The Prints of Roy Lichtenstein: a catalogue raisonné 1948–1993*, New York: Hudson Hills Press in association with the National Gallery of Art, Washington, 1994, cat nos III 20 and III 21 respectively, p. 272.
21. Roy Lichtenstein, in *Reaching Out: Ken Tyler, master printer* (documentary film), Avery Tirce Productions, 1976.
22. ibid.
23. Ken Tyler, Qantas Birthday Lecture, 14 October 1999, National Gallery of Australia, Canberra.
24. John Coplans, 'Talking with Roy Lichtenstein', in John Coplans (ed.), *Roy Lichtenstein*, London: Allen Lane, the Penguin Press, 1973, p. 88.
25. ibid., p. 89.
26. David Sylvester, *Some Kind of Reality: Roy Lichtenstein interviewed by David Sylvester* (exhibition catalogue), London: Anthony D'Offray Gallery, 1997, quoted in *Roy Lichtenstein* (exhibition catalogue), Basel: Fondation Beyler, 1998, p. 54.
27. Ken Tyler, correspondence with Jane Kinsman, 11 June 2002.
28. Michael Kimmelman, *Portraits: talking with artists at the Met, the Modern, the Louvre and elsewhere*, New York: the Modern Library, 1999, p. 89.

A Moving Focus

David Hockney

Of the many artists who have collaborated with Ken Tyler in his various workshops over the years, only David Hockney has worked in all four of them. Hockney found a printer who was both technically innovative and extraordinarily active. 'Working with someone who has an awful lot of energy is very thrilling. With Ken Tyler nothing was impossible. If I said, could we, he said, yes, yes, it can be done.'[1]

Hockney was born in Bradford, England, in 1937. To this day he has kept the strong accent and humour of the Yorkshireman, even though he has spent many years, on and off, living in America — where some of his most exciting prints have been made. He is a consummate printmaker, for whom the discovery of a new technique, a new method of printmaking, often will serve as a catalyst to create a new artistic focus:

I love new mediums … I think mediums can turn you on, they can excite you: they always let you do something in a different way, even if you take the same subject, if you draw it in a different way, or if you are forced to simplify it, to make it bold because it is too finicky. I like that .[2]

It was at the Tamarind Lithography Workshop that Tyler first met Hockney in March 1964, when the artist was visiting California. 'He was making a guest print titled Pacific Mutual Life Building with palm tree', Tyler remembers.

Shortly thereafter I met Paul Cornwall Jones, the London publisher of Editions Alecto, who had an exclusive contract on David's prints. I also met John Kasmin of Kasmin Gallery in London. These two were the key players in David's graphic work at the time along with Henry Geldzahler [curator of the twentieth-century art department at the Metropolitan Museum of Art, New York], who served as editor and advisor to David. David was hanging out in California when I opened my shop in September 1965 in the back of Jerry Solomon's frame shop.

Paul wanted David to work with me so he could get more prints of David's to sell. Knowing that David and I most likely would work in colour, Paul was keen on David doing a serious project with me. The brightness of LA light contributed to the colorful series A Hollywood Collection. At the time, I only had facilities for lithography. David liked the idea that he was supporting a young printer and the atmosphere in the 'Art Services' building was for him interesting. He got to meet actors, collectors and artists at the frame shop and hang out at the restaurants and galleries around Melrose Ave. By this time David was a celebrity in LA. He also thought I was a pretty good printer![3]

Hockney recalls that he was drawn to Los Angeles because it was 'nice and warm' and 'always sunny'.

Which means it is always sexy. Which means light, full of colour … I just had a hunch it was a place I'd like. I just went there; I didn't know a soul there. I thought it was three times better than I imagined when I got there.[4]

A COLLECTION FOR HOLLYWOOD

The first group of prints Tyler and Hockney made together was a set of six colour lithographs, *A Hollywood Collection* 1965, at the Gemini Ltd workshop on Melrose Avenue in Los Angeles. Hockney had not made lithographs since he editioned three colour prints while he was a schoolboy in Bradford. Subsequently he worked in etching, which he found less cumbersome and more

(opposite) David Hockney drawing 'Celia' on lithographic stone, 1973, Gemini GEL (photograph Daniel Freeman)

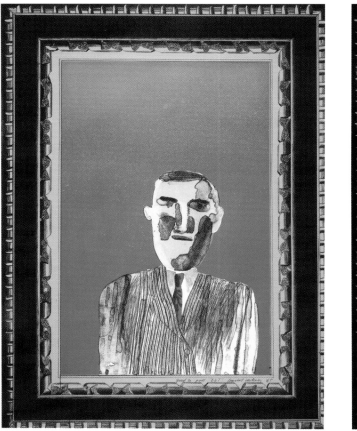

immediate. It was not until he made lithographs with Tyler that he could explore the potential of that medium. *A Hollywood Collection* is a witty group of compositions in bold colours not seen before in Hockney's printmaking. The combination of bright colour and the mixture of flat and rounded forms owes something to his painting style, since he began painting in synthetic polymer paint after he moved to Los Angeles. Each print is in the form of a different genre of painting — a still life, a landscape, a portrait, a cityscape, a nude and an abstract — an instant art collection. The genres are also shown in a variety of styles, from a Cubist variation and an abstract form, to a figure drawn in a manner recollecting the naïve drawing of Dubuffet (an early influence on Hockney) and so on. One has a painterly tree set against a flat sky; another has a painterly sky, with the stark flat form of a building in the foreground.

David HOCKNEY
from *A Hollywood Collection* colour lithographs 1965
(opposite from top left to bottom right)
Picture of a Still Life that has an Elaborate Silver Frame
Picture of a Landscape in an Elaborate Gold Frame
Picture of a Portrait in a Silver Frame
Picture of Melrose Avenue in an Ornate Gold Frame
(above left to right) **Picture of a Simple Framed Traditional Nude Drawing**
Picture of a Pointless Abstraction Framed under Glass

Despite the melange of styles, these compositions were nevertheless unified. As part of the composition Hockney 'framed' each work with a different design, ranging from the ornamental to a more simple modernist frame. These witty inclusions were inspired by his workplace surroundings: 'Gemini … was behind a frame-maker's shop, and that's why I did the frames as part of the prints.'[5]

51

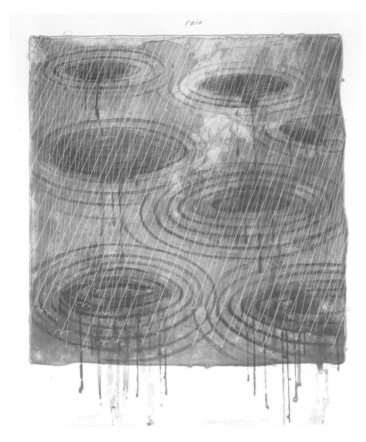

THE SUBJECT IS DRAWING

After making *A Hollywood Collection* in 1965 and then a single print *Sofa 8501 Hedges Place* in 1971, Hockney and Tyler didn't collaborate again until 1973, a watershed year for the artist. It was at this point that he realised his painting was trapped in naturalism. An invitation to work at Gemini GEL gave him the opportunity to escape this artistic rut, and in January he arrived at the workshop. 'I had been trying to get David to work again over the years', Tyler remembers, 'and at long last he decided to work.'

His usual entourage [of Celia Birtwell and Henry Geldzahler] was with him during his yearly visit to southern California … They stayed both at the Chateau Marmount Hotel and in Malibu. David held court at the new workshop and worked off and on from January to April 1973. He also had a very important role in the filming by Jack Glenn and Sid Avery of their film on me titled 'Reaching Out' in the first week of April, 1973. Celia Smoking was the featured print.[6]

Hockney was given a 'complete palette of colour' and a 'complete palette of drawing techniques'.[7] He had never been offered such a comprehensive range of options

before, and went on to produce a group of accomplished and sometimes witty prints. He became set on the idea of a weather series, beginning with *Rain*, a print inspired by Japanese woodcuts. He had already explored the theme of rain in his painting *The Japanese Rain on Canvas* of 1972 — his response to Japan after a trip there in November 1971.

Although Hockney's preconceptions of Japan were shattered — he found it 'extremely ugly'[8] — what did engage him during his stay was an exhibition, *Japanese Painters in the Traditional Style*, in Kyoto, and in particular a picture, *Osaka in the Rain*.

I thought it exceedingly beautiful. The misty clouds over the river and street were suggested only by the thin bars of rain, and the little cars and people walking about all had just the slightest suggestion of reflection under them, making the whole thing look extremely wet.[9]

David HOCKNEY
from *Weather* series 1973 colour lithographs, screenprints
(above left) **Rain**
(above right) **Sun**
(opposite left) **Wind**
(opposite right) **Snow**

Hockney painted *The Japanese Rain on Canvas* on his return to London. Its title is almost literal, as the artist explained: 'The picture is painted in thin washes of colour soaked on to the canvas and, because I was anxious to make the heavily stylised falling rain stand out, I filled a watering-can and let it drip all over the canvas.'[10] Continuing this idea, with the colour lithograph *Rain*, from the *Weather* series, Hockney dripped ink onto a lithographic stone. In the documentary film *Reaching Out*, he commented: 'I did it kind of as a joke really. I loved the idea of the rain as it hit the ink. It would make the ink run. The moment I thought of the idea I couldn't resist it.' He then turned his attention to other ideas relating to the weather theme, inventing the series as he proceeded, and drawing on the Japanese ukiyo-e print imagery of such artists as Hokusai and Hiroshige.

The point really was that as the prints grew, the subject matter which on the surface is the weather, but the other subject matter is really the weather drawn. Because in each one the problem was, not just making a representation of the weather, but how to draw it. I liked the problem of how to draw a mist.

The one thing I didn't really want to do was spray it: you know, it's too easy … At first I wanted to do it with light, just ruling the light. And it didn't really quite work. In the end we designed some ways to do it. But it was finding out … ways of doing it. It means that the subject of the prints is not just the weather: the subject matter is drawing.[11]

For *Wind*, Hockney said: 'I couldn't quite figure out how … to make a visual representation of wind, because normally only the effects of wind show themselves. So I kept thinking of palm trees bending and everything and it all seemed just a little bit corny or ordinary.' He solved the problem one day at Malibu beach, while watching a paper tossed in the wind: 'It suddenly dawned on me. I'll simply do all the other prints I've done blowing away across Melrose Avenue.'[12] In this composition he refers to Tyler's Gemini GEL address, just as he had included the old workshop location in the *A Hollywood Collection* series in 1965 (the larger premises was further along Melrose Avenue).

54

PRIVATE WORLD

Following the *Weather* series, Hockney turned to portraiture. This superb draughtsman is noted for his sensitive, beautifully rendered portraits of lovers, family and friends. Rarely does he make portraits of those he has not met before — in one such instance, in September 1973, the well-known Bradford-born writer J.B. Priestley sat for a portrait, which the artist felt obliged to do. Hockney spoke of his reluctance:

It's more difficult drawing people you don't know. It's more difficult in a pointless way I think, because first of all I feel obliged to get a likeness, which in a sense is easy to do, it's easy to draw a likeness, but it may not be that easy to capture a certain mood of somebody or things like that, which in a way is more interesting … You know all you need to do to draw a likeness is to be able to measure the proportion of the face accurately with your eyes, that's all. It's not that difficult.[13]

David HOCKNEY
(opposite) **Celia Smoking** 1973 lithograph
(left) **Celia** 1973 lithograph
(above) **Celia in a Black Dress with Red Stockings** 1973 coloured crayon drawing

In February 1973, Hockney rented a house at Malibu where Celia Birtwell and her children came to stay. Hockney began a series of lithographic portraits of Celia — a particular favourite and a special muse whom he had drawn many times. The range and subtlety of the washes he could achieve at the workshop were of a kind that Hockney had never been offered before, and drawing directly onto the stone or plate suited him. With *Celia Smoking*, on occasions Tyler 'invaded David's very private world'[14] to facilitate the artist's working.

I took it upon myself to offer a suggestion at a very critical moment, because (a) it is brilliant work, and (b) it happens to be somebody who put a tremendous amount of effort into making the best lithographs we could, and he's capable of doing just a simple drawing and it's brilliant.

… what you do is you just pull out your reservoir of techniques and say, 'Wash it off, because we can add it here, we can do this, you can do that, we can cut the shoulder off because you can redraw it again five times if you want to. You know, there's a lot of things that you can do' … I just had to volunteer the information, regardless of how he was going to accept it … And unless we did that little surgical operation, I don't think there would have been a Celia Smoking. Nor would Celia Smoking have looked like that, and that's what I love about the business, is that you always have this opportunity to help.[15]

Hockney felt secure that the quality of his drawing would not be lost: Tyler would 'make sure everything you put there stays there, which is not that easy, especially if you've used delicate washes, thin crayon, things like that'.[16]

These portraits of Celia are notable for their intimacy, and this closeness between artist and model continued later that year in Paris, where Hockney made a further series of portraits of her. 'The only time it came near to being a sexual thing was when I went to Paris', Celia recalled.

And he did drawings of me in negligées. It was like something was going on, but it was quite remote … In the French drawings, when we were very close, there was something going on between us which I think he portrayed through those drawings. He said to me that this was his way of expressing how he felt about me.[17]

During his stay at Gemini GEL in 1973, Hockney made other lithographic portraits. Tyler sat for him, and the artist did a small lithograph of Henry Geldzahler, executed rapidly. In contrast, the formal portrait of Tyler, *The Master Printer of Los Angeles*, took two days of posing. There is a picture within that picture — in the background, *Rain*, from the *Weather* series, appears on the wall. Similarly, the Hiroshige inspired landscape of *Snow* appears in the background in one Celia portrait.

David HOCKNEY
(below left) **Celia, 8365 Melrose Avenue, Hollywood** 1973 lithograph, crayon
(below right) **The Master Printer of Los Angeles [Portrait of Kenneth Tyler]** 1973 colour lithograph, screenprint

PAPER WORK

After Tyler had moved to Bedford, upstate New York, establishing Tyler Workshop Ltd in 1974, he repeatedly tried to encourage Hockney to visit. Then in 1978, while Hockney was on a return trip from England to Los Angeles, he stopped over in New York to arrange the necessary paperwork after losing his driver's licence. While waiting for this to be processed Hockney visited the printer in Bedford.

Since his time at Tamarind, Tyler had harboured a passion for handmade paper, and he developed a growing expertise in its making. Because so many of the artists with whom he worked over the years were able to explore new ways of making prints, Tyler saw another important role for himself in providing the kinds of paper which would support these exploratory ventures. The large sheets required by Rauschenberg and his experimental paper works are early examples of this.

In Tyler's Bedford years, his great love of handmade paper particularly came to the fore. Since moving to the east coast, he had worked with John Koller at his HMP mill in Connecticut, but the workshop's constant focus on experimentation, using paper pulp on a large scale, meant that their requirements quickly outgrew this small mill. Tyler then established his own papermaking facilities in the garage of the Bedford workshop, mixing different fibres and eastern and western papermaking techniques.

On that visit in 1978, Hockney saw the works made of paper pulp by Ellsworth Kelly and Kenneth Noland and thought them 'stunningly beautiful … especially Ellsworth Kelly's'.[18] At the time, Hockney had not been interested in making further graphic works, wanting rather to paint and be on his own. But he decided to stay for a few days, curious about the possibilities of paper pulp — although initially he was very tentative:

I said, I love using lines, Ken, I'm not very good at using colour, bold colour, I'm too timid with it really … I was drawing sunflowers; I drew the leaves on the stems, and then

Ken said he would make a mould [which held the paper pulp] of just the leaves first, and I could draw in the stems myself. We made the moulds and then I looked at it and I realized that you didn't really need the stem at all.[19]

Flowers were a favourite motif of Hockney's and the palette of his first paper piece was reminiscent of Vincent van Gogh's sunflowers. Van Gogh's painting was one of the artist's favourites at the National Gallery in London, and one of his four treasured reproductions of that work featured in his painting of Geldzahler, *Looking at Pictures on a Screen* of 1976. The National Gallery went on to exhibit this Hockney painting with the van Gogh, and Hockney's other favourite works by Piero della Francesca, Vermeer and Degas; and the artist wrote an essay on these much-loved works, which was published in 1981.[20]

David Hockney applying coloured pulp to a section of a 12-panel *Paper Pool*, '*A Diver*' 1978, Bedford (photograph Jill Sabella)

58

As the days at Bedford passed, Hockney allowed the process to lead him into new avenues. In the end the artist stayed for 49 days, working 16 hours a day with just one day off (Tyler counted the days, Hockney did not). From August to October of 1978, Hockney made a series of 29 paper works with Tyler and assistant Lindsay Green. The subject became the swimming pool.

I kept looking at the swimming pool; and it's a wonderful subject, water, the light on the water. And this process with paper pulp demanded a lot of water; I thought, really I should do, find a watery subject for this process, and here it is; here, this pool, every time that you look at the surface, you look through it, you look under it.[21]

The pool, the light and shadows on the water, the steps, and the diving board, and later with the effect on it of different times of day and seasonal changes were all examined by Hockney in these changing circumstances just as Claude Monet had done nearly a century before. To assist his process, Hockney took multiple polaroids of the subject, as well as drawing it. He stopped considering papermaking as a graphic medium and began to 'paint' with colour paper pulp, using galvanised cookie cutter moulds to make the shapes, and turkey basters and other implements such as spoons to poor or squirt on the dye. The sheet would be half pressed, squeezing out some of the water and leaving it moist, so that Hockney could add further colour, enlivening the work. He would dart back and forth like a painter touching up a canvas. 'Gradually I realised that you could work with moulds, as if "drawing" the form … and pour all the colours next to one another'.[22] It is interesting to note how Hockney's involvement in paper pulp making assisted his broader artistic development, and that he now became notable for his gift as a colourist — a latter-day Matisse.

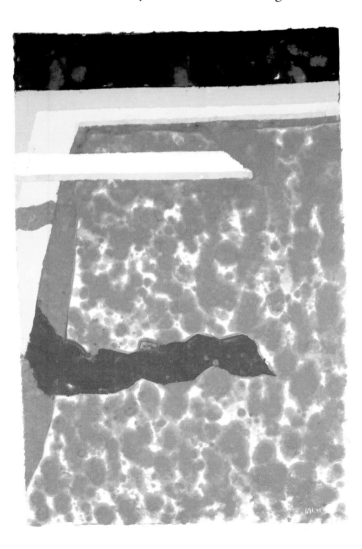

David HOCKNEY
(opposite) **Steps with Shadow, Paper Pool 2-H** 1978
hand-coloured and pressed coloured paper pulp
(left) **Green Pool with Diving Board and Shadow, Paper Pool 3-I** 1978
hand-coloured and pressed coloured paper pulp
(below) **Ken Tyler** 1978 sepia ink

Finding the medium such a bold one, Hockney began to envisage works on a bigger scale, and placed a number of mould-made sheets together, first six and then 12. His last group of three *Paper Pools,* each on 12 sheets, reveals Hockney's interest in depicting a figure as it moves through water, and the splash of the body as it enters the pool from the board. With Hockney, experimentation and innovation in paperwork became an obsession.

During his stay at Bedford Village, there were times when the artist had to sit on the sidelines; and on those occasions he made ink drawings — using a reed pen similar to one used by van Gogh — of Tyler and Green, either at work or taking a brief moment's rest, the workshop, and the pool.

David HOCKNEY
(above) **A Diver, Paper Pool 17** 1978 hand-coloured and pressed coloured paper pulp
(following pages) **Gregory Swimming, Los Angeles, 31 March 1982**
1982 composite polaroid

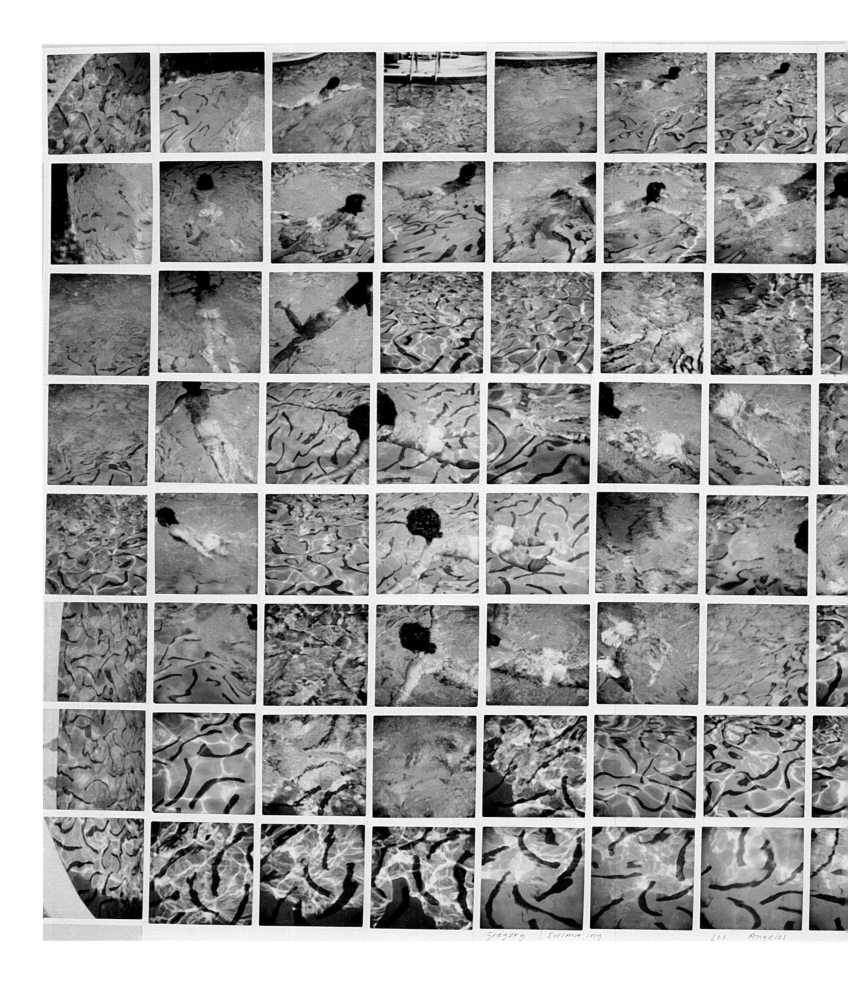

Gregory Swimming.   Los Angeles

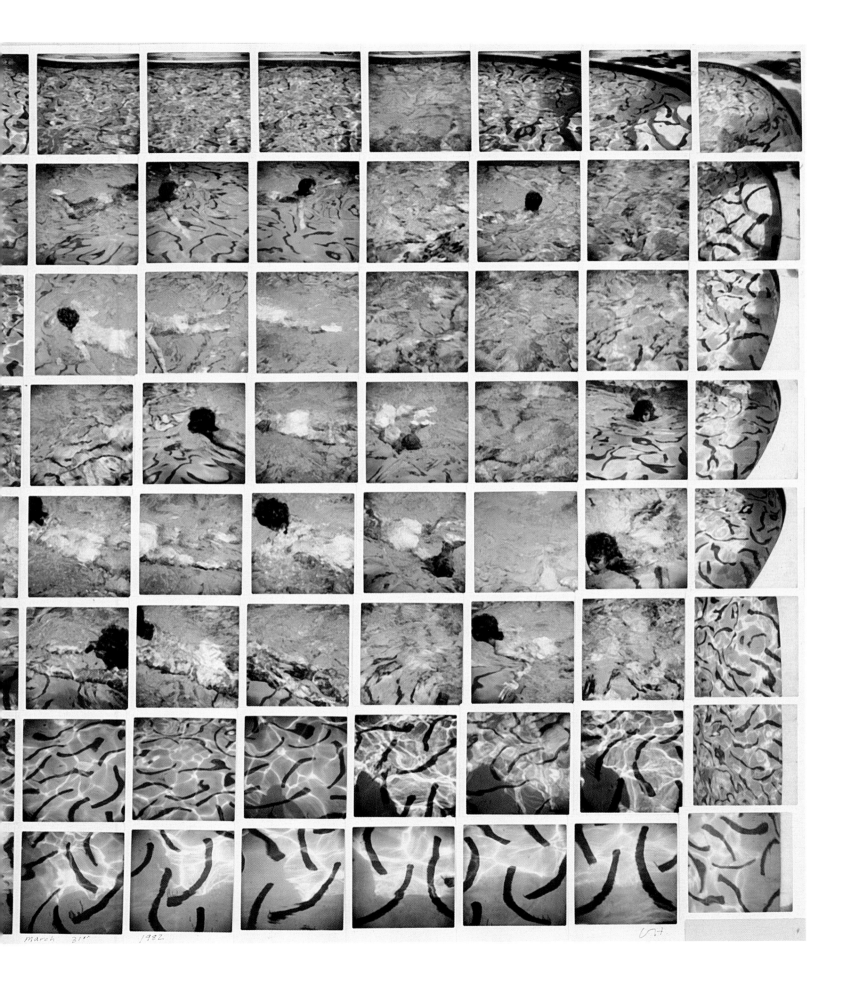

March 31st   1982

EN PLEIN AIR

In the mid-1980s, Hockney made a series of 29 prints in colour lithography consisting of interior views and chairs in reverse perspective, views of a Mexican hotel, and portraits, including collaged portraits of Celia Birtwell and the artist's partner, Gregory Evans. Titled the *Moving Focus* series, it was a summation of Hockney's obsession with space at that time — the depiction of space, the experience of being within a space, or travelling through space over time. Many of these prints were made during 1984–85, when Hockney worked at Bedford Village while his house in Los Angeles was being renovated. *Moving Focus* is notable for its innovation, both technically and compositionally, with the works stretching the boundaries of lithography and exploring multipoint perspective. In this series the artist drew from the lessons he learned while studying Cubism closely, particularly the work of Picasso, a lifelong interest.

By 1978, Hockney had a complete collection of the Zervos volumes — all 32 of them — which published Picasso's oeuvre in painting and drawing, and which was like a 'gigantic diary' that Hockney could study.[23] He saw Picasso's work, particularly in Cubism, not as a distortion but more real than naturalism. You no longer looked at the picture, 'you were *inside* the picture; you had to be, because you couldn't be simply outside it and move round it'.[24] Hockney's tribute to Picasso — the artist he considered

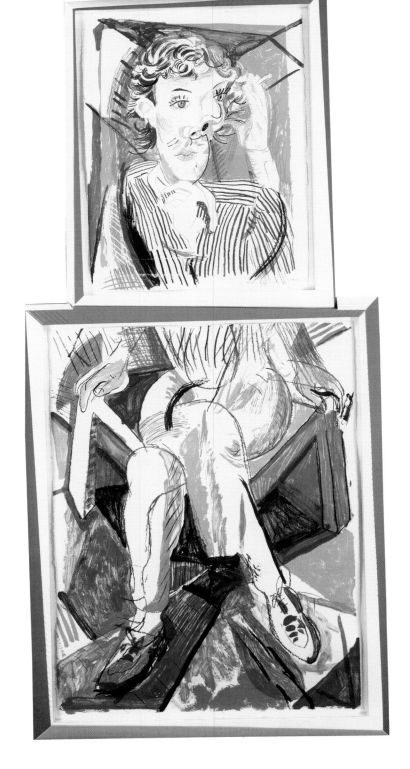

David HOCKNEY from *Moving Focus* series 1984–87
(above) **An Image of Gregory** 1985 colour lithograph, collage on two sheets, handpainted frame
(opposite) **An Image of Celia** 1986 colour lithograph, screenprint, collage, handpainted frame

the most significant of the twentieth century — can be seen in *Paint Trolley, L.A., 1985,* a multifaceted collage of photographs that each have one-point perspective but which, combined, provide a multipoint reverse perspective. To complete his homage, Hockney placed his treasured volumes of Zervos in the composition with his own paints, brushes, and his portrait head of Celia used for the cover of the Paris *Vogue* Christmas 1985 issue which he designed.

There were other lessons learned in Hockney's exploration of space. One of the most exciting experiences of his life was the day he saw a great Chinese painted scroll at the Metropolitan Museum's Department of Far Eastern Art. Within the continuous landscape of the scroll, different

times are depicted simultaneously, with the multiple viewpoints of buildings and streetscapes coalescing to form a greater sense of the subject than is possible with a scene represented from a one-point perspective. 'How marvellously it dealt with space, time and narrative … I had just been through a Chinese city; I'd spent hours wandering up one street, down another, up another, and I was not fixed in one point.'[25] Hockney's own experience, designing sets for operatic productions, also contributed to his escape from what he termed 'obsessive naturalism' and into an investigation of alternative depictions of space.

David HOCKNEY
(opposite) **An Image of Celia, State I** 1984–86 colour lithograph
from *Moving Focus* series 1984–87
(above) **Paint Trolley, L.A., 1985** 1985 photographic collage

The idea for the major theme of the *Moving Focus* series came from Hockney's experience in Mexico, when he attended the opening of the exhibition *Hockney Paints the Stage*, in February 1984. On the way from Mexico City to Oaxaca, the artist's car broke down and Hockney, with Gregory Evans and David Graves were stranded in the little town of Acatlán. There they stayed at the Hotel Romano Angeles while repairs were under way. The artist was captivated by the hotel and its garden: 'The hotel courtyard was very beautiful and I made a number of

sketches there towards an oil painting.' As well as various sketches of the hotel, he photographed it. The intended works were not to be 'about a hotel, but about an attitude to space'.[26] Indeed, in the lithographs that resulted Hockney continued to explore reverse perspective. The space is empty, except for the occasional reference to a human presence. He began to use this method of creating reverse perspective with his painting *Kerby (after Hogarth) Useful Knowledge* of 1975.

$\frac{1}{98}$

David HOCKNEY from *Moving Focus* series 1984–87
(opposite) **Tyler Dining Room** 1985 colour lithograph
(above) **Two Pembroke Studio Chairs** 1984 colour lithograph

On his return to Los Angeles, Hockney spoke to Tyler about his Mexican experience, and Tyler saw this as an opportunity to work outside the confines of a studio. 'For years I have thought it would be nice to … do a project outside the shop in print making, as we have always done with making multiples and I have discussed this many times with David.' It was a chance to work with Hockney using a mylar lithographic technique he had been perfecting, which would allow the artist to work *en plein air* in the manner of the Impressionists, and Tyler flew to California to demonstrate it.

Mylar was used as the drawing surface, from which the image could be then be directly transferred to a photosensitive lithographic plate. Hockney enthusiastically embraced it, as Tyler recalls:

He drew a seven-colour print depicting the interior of his painting studio, placing each drawn sheet over the preceding colour one. With each successive mylar sheet he seemed to introduce new layers of experimentation, wetting colour crayons to create washes on the mylar, drawing on the mylar over textures, or scraping into drawn areas with a razor blade. David has always had a keen sense of process and a knack for bypassing established methodologies to arrive at previously undiscovered uses for new materials and techniques.[27]

It was to be a perfect technique for Hockney, as the artist was adept at thinking in layers and warmed to experimentation. The transparent nature of mylar allowed him to view all the different coloured marks on the combined sheets at one glance.

The mylar technique also made the printing process easier. Tyler wrote: 'Since 1980 I had been developing a new technique for continuous-tone lithography: the plates were printed on a flat-bed offset press using hand-drawn positives made on clear and translucent

David **HOCKNEY** from *Moving Focus* series 1984–87
(above) **Walking Past Two Chairs** 1984 colour lithograph, screenprint, hand painted frame
(opposite) **Amaryllis in Vase** 1985 colour lithograph

plastic, coated acetate and mylar sheets.' This was a great innovation in colour lithography. The traditional practice had been to print first in black before colour. Then each colour used had to be traced separately onto different plates, which also meant making many proofs.

The drawn mylars were made into plates and went directly to press for colour proofing. We soon learned how to process colour drawings on plastic sheets, exploiting a variety of oil-paint sticks and water-soluble crayons which could be diluted to create watercolour effects. For the first time, acetate and mylar sheets could be drawn with colour crayons to make individual printing plates. Since they were already in registration, tracings onto additional plates were not necessary. The colour separations were stacked on top of each other, granting the artist the freedom of going back and forth to correct any passages of the drawing by addition or subtraction. Even after proofing, the original drawn mylars could be corrected and new plates made.[28]

After some initial experimentation with the artist, Tyler travelled with Hockney when he returned to the hotel at Acatlán. There the artist worked on the mylar sheets, producing a series of compositions of the hotel courtyard.

David HOCKNEY from *Moving Focus* series 1984–87
(above) **Views of Hotel Well I** 1985 colour lithograph with hand-painted frame
(opposite) **Views of Hotel Well III** 1984–85 colour lithograph with hand-painted frame

73

74

David HOCKNEY Hotel, Acatlán: Two Weeks Later 1985
colour lithograph on two sheets from *Moving Focus* series 1984–87

Tyler's romantic notions of the Hotel Romano Angeles were soon dispelled — to his astonishment, there was not a real brick in sight; rather, the walls and the fountain in the courtyard were made of painted plaster. To complete the scene, the household plumbing ran into the courtyard and watered the garden.

The last of the *Moving Focus* series was the screen, *Caribbean Tea Time* of 1987 — a celebratory scene composed by Hockney in recollection of a recent holiday on Mustique. As with many of the series, it had its own handpainted frame and,

as in the other views in reverse perspective, the composition did not contain a human figure. As the artist explained, the viewer of the work was intended to be the human element. The screen comprises eight panels of handmade paper printed with colour lithography and screenprinting, in brilliant colours worthy of Matisse.

For Tyler, the mylar technique, 'while providing the artist with a more immediate process for making and correcting colour prints … saved the workshop hundreds of hours of processing.'

Within the first year of the Moving Focus project, the workshop had used the technique to proof and print some 293 colour plates. By its completion, the project had used a total of 577 colour plates. For such extensive work, the traditional colour lithography process would have taken the workshop nearly three times as long.[29]

The *Moving Focus* series also stands as an important investigation into ideas about representing space and time. As Hockney explained: 'In these prints there is no way to see what is depicted all at once.'

Your eyes have to move over the surface of the paper. In doing that you're very aware that you keep moving from one thing to another and in your mind you convert that time to space

… Space can be made into time. That's the way space is created in these pictures, because there's many perspectives. If there's only one-point perspective, there's only one moment in time. That's why it restricts space, because one moment in time has put a boundary on space.[30]

The series points to future developments in the work of this artist, notably in the brilliantly coloured 60-canvas painting *A Bigger Grand Canyon* of 1998. This painting evolved over a decade with the artist's growing obsession with space explored through photocollages, theatre design and landscape painting. *A Bigger Grand Canyon*, now in the collection of the National Gallery of Australia, is a culminating statement by the artist about the depiction of space, and the experience of being within a space, or travelling through a space, over time. For Hockney, working on the *Moving Focus* series was crucial to such explorations.

Notes

1. David Hockney, quoted in Nikos Stangos (ed.), *David Hockney: Paper Pools,* London: Thames and Hudson, 1980, p. 100.
2. ibid.
3. Ken Tyler, correspondence with Jane Kinsman, 29 May 2002.
4. David Hockney, in *David Hockney at the Tate* (documentary film), London: Phaedon, produced and directed by Alan Benson, London, 1988.
5. David Hockney, *David Hockney by David Hockney*, London: Thames and Hudson, 1976, p. 101.
6. Ken Tyler, correspondence with Jane Kinsman, 26 July 2002.
7. Ken Tyler, in *Reaching Out: Ken Tyler, master printer* (documentary film), Avery Tirce Productions, 1976.
8. David Hockney, *David Hockney by David Hockney*, London: Thames and Hudson, 1976, p. 242.
9. ibid.
10. ibid., p. 247.
11. David Hockney, in *Reaching Out: Ken Tyler, master printer* (documentary film), Avery Tirce Productions, 1976.
12. ibid.
13. ibid.
14. ibid.
15. Ken Tyler, in *Reaching Out: Ken Tyler, master printer* (documentary film), Avery Tirce Productions, 1976.
16. David Hockney, quoted in Ruth E. Fine, *Gemini GEL: art and collaboration*, Washington: National Gallery of Art; New York: Abbeville Press, 1984, p. 146.
17. Peter Webb, *Portrait of David Hockney*, London: Chatto & Windus, 1988, p. 135.
18. David Hockney, quoted in Nikos Stangos (ed.), *David Hockney: Paper Pools,* London: Thames and Hudson, 1980, p. 10, see note 1.
19. ibid., p. 21.
20. David Hockney, *Looking at Pictures in a Book at the National Gallery*, London: The National Gallery, 1981.
21. Nikos Stangos (ed.), *David Hockney: Paper Pools,* London: Thames and Hudson, 1980, p. 21.
22. ibid.
23. David Hockney, *That's the Way I See It*, ed. Nikos Stangos, London: Thames and Hudson, 1993, p. 115; Greek-born writer Christian Zervos was a friend of Picasso's. He devoted much of his life from 1932 to 1978 to editing and publishing a catalogue of Picasso's paintings and drawings (*Pablo Picasso*, Paris: Cahiers d'art, 1932–1978).
24. David Hockney, *That's the Way I See It*, Nikos Stangos (ed.), London: Thames and Hudson, 1993, p. 102.
25. ibid., p. 128.
26. ibid., p. 157.
27. Ken Tyler, 'Layers of Space and Time: David Hockney's *Moving Focus*', in *Contemporary Master Prints from the Lilja Collection*, Liechtenstein and London: the Lilja Art Fund Foundation in association with Azimuth Editions Limited, 1995, p. 123.
28. ibid., p. 121.
29. ibid., p. 123.
30. Interview with Pat Gilmour at Tyler Graphics Ltd, Bedford, New York, 22 June 1985, quoted in Ken Tyler, 'Layers of Space and Time: David Hockney's *Moving Focus*', in *Contemporary Master Prints from the Lilja Collection*, Liechtenstein and London: the Lilja Art Fund Foundation in association with Azimuth Editions Limited, 1995, p. 124.

(opposite above) David Hockney drawing Gregory Evans, 1984, Tyler Graphics Ltd, Bedford Village (photograph Kenneth Tyler)
(opposite below) Celia Birtwell poses for David Hockney as he begins preliminary drawings for *An Image of Celia*, artist's studio at Tyler Graphics Ltd, November 1984 (photograph Kenneth Tyler)

The Painterly Print
Robert Motherwell

Over the years Ken Tyler has worked with the divergent styles of many artists, adapting to the particular requirements of each. With David Hockney, for example, the challenge was to develop new techniques and processes to maintain the artist's interest. Producing 'painterly prints' for major Abstract Expressionist artists Robert Motherwell and Helen Frankenthaler was also a considerable challenge. For these artists, who both work in an intuitive automatic manner, the technicalities of printmaking could be seen as a constraint. Yet in their collaborative work with Tyler, both maintained the freshness of their expression, despite the rigours of production.

THE SCHOOL OF PARIS

Robert Motherwell acquired his love of modern art early in his life. This passion began with Cézanne, followed by Matisse, then Picasso. An element that united these artists, and other French artists of the Impressionist period, is that they all worked in Provence at some time during their careers and, of course, that is where Cézanne was born and chose to live for much of his life. Motherwell felt that he had an affinity with them because he shared the experience of living in a landscape dominated by strong light and shadows, and earth colours — the California of his childhood. There he 'grew up in a landscape not at all dissimilar to Provence, or to the central plateau of Spain, or to parts of Italy and the Mediterranean basin … edges are sharp, shadows are black.'[1]

Following his studies in California, Motherwell accompanied his father to Europe in 1935, and the experience stimulated his interest in other cultures. Although his wealthy family expected him to take up a profession, Motherwell was keen to become an artist, and came to an agreement with his father that, if he studied philosophy at university, he would receive a regular stipend. He then entered the graduate school of arts and sciences at Harvard. The topic of his doctoral dissertation was 'The journals of Eugène Delacroix' (whose work he admired). In a deft move, Motherwell managed to spend 15 months painting in France during his Harvard years. He then moved to New York to further his studies at Columbia University, under the renowned art historian, Professor Meyer Schapiro.

THE SCHOOL OF NEW YORK

Motherwell was searching for inspiration, and Schapiro proposed that he should get in touch with the European Surrealists then living in New York — among them Max Ernst, Roberto Matta, Marcel Duchamp and André Masson. Recalling this time, Motherwell reflected on their displacement:

I had come to New York in 1940, after a year in Paris. Through a number of coincidences, the first significant artists I knew professionally were … Europeans in exile … One of the many difficulties for [them], particularly the ones who didn't speak English very well, was the lack of public meeting places. Most of these artists spent their life in Paris with its café life and New York City was so different.[2]

In New York they congregated at various cafés, bookshops and galleries, including Peggy Guggenheim's Art of this Century Gallery. It was through his association with the Surrealists that Motherwell was able to clarify his thoughts about the way forward for American art, not only in terms of style, but also method. At Schapiro's behest, the Surrealist artist Kurt Seligmann proposed that Motherwell study engraving with him at his New York studio.

(opposite)
Robert MOTHERWELL
Elegy to the Spanish Republic 1958 synthetic polymer paint on canvas

Another location for émigrés in New York was Stanley William Hayter's Atelier 17, an intaglio print workshop whose house style was more modernist than figurative, and where Motherwell made etchings. Until that time, he had been somewhat reticent about printmaking, a practice he associated with artists of little consequence. Despite being surrounded by European artists of great talent who were well versed in printing, Motherwell quit Atelier 17 because of what he considered to be the studio's overemphasis on technical matters. On the postwar period he commented:

There is still a kind of cold war between the old guard, constantly talking about how you technically do or complicate works in any way possible, and artists who simply have a statement they want to make as clearly and as forcibly as they can, within the nature of this particular medium.[3]

It was an environment that did not lend itself to Motherwell's making of art. For him the key collaboration was between art and artist.

The subject does not pre-exist. It emerges out of the interaction between the artist and the medium. That is why, and only how [my work] can be created, and why its conclusion cannot be predetermined. When [one has] a predetermined conclusion, you have 'academic art' by definition ... An artistic medium, which is not an inert object, or, conversely, a set of rules for composition, but a living collaboration, which not only reflects every nuance of one's being but which, in the moment in which one is 'lost', comes to one's aid ... as when a canvas says to one, 'This empty space in me needs to be pinker'; or a shape says, 'I want to be larger and more expansive'; or the format says, 'The conception is too large or too small for me, all out of scale'; or a stripe says, 'Gouge me more, you are too polite and elegant'; or a gray says, 'A bit more blue — my present color is uncomfortable and does not fit.'[4]

AN AUTOMATIC ARM AND A MODERN STILL LIFE

One of Motherwell's methods of working was derived from the Surrealist theory of psychic automatism, or free association. In 1942 he discussed the theory with Jackson Pollock and experimented with writing poetry in that manner. It was Motherwell's view that 'the art scene was parochial' at that time in America: 'No one thought that we could ever produce truly great modern painting: only Europeans could. So we had nothing to lose by risking all.'[5] He felt that modern American artists had to seek a creative principle that would lead them away from a mannered adherence to European styles. This principle should involve the Surrealists' psychic automatism. An American art, however, should favour huge scale, enormous energy and sheer daring:

for us, certain Surrealist methods were means for arriving at painting as painting ... Abstract Expressionism also went beyond art ... as a vision of its own, profoundly different in weight, drive, and frankness from the fantasy, dreaminess, satire and black humour of the Surrealists.[6]

One way Motherwell responded to the challenge of establishing a truly American art was by developing archetypal imagery. From 1948, he began his *Elegies to the Spanish Republic,* first in painting and later in printmaking. The images, evoking the tragic past, and the defeat of the democratically elected Republicans by the Monarchists in the 1930s civil war in his much-loved Spain, would stay with him for his lifetime.

The reason I've made so many works ... is simply because I feel that I've never fully resolved any of them. They remain an endless challenge. The day I can make an Elegy that really satisfies me, perhaps then I'll stop that search.[7]

For Motherwell to succeed in this cerebral process, Tyler commented, 'His *automatic arm* has to be working just right before it comes out'.[8]

Another method favoured by Motherwell was collage, which he considered as an equivalent to a modern still life; and his collage work serves as a journal outlining his development. From a distance of almost 40 years he reflected on how important collage had become to

Robert MOTHERWELL
(opposite above) **Lament for Lorca** 1982 lithograph
(opposite below) Robert Motherwell observes as Kenneth Tyler and Lee Funderburg pull an impression of **Lament for Lorca** 1982, Tyler Graphics Ltd, Bedford Village
(photograph Lindsay Green)

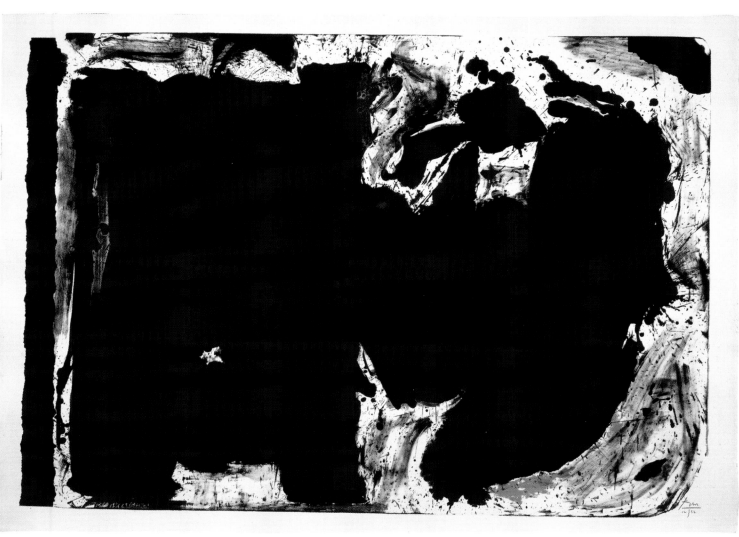

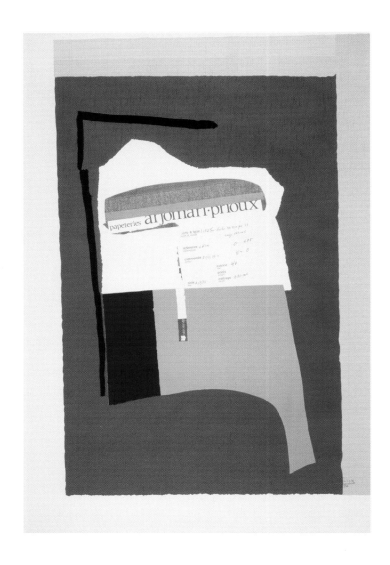

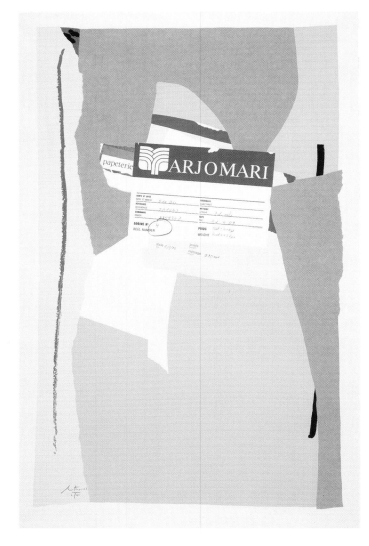

Robert MOTHERWELL
from the series *America-La France Variations* 1983–84
colour lithographs, collage on TGL handmade paper
(left to right) **Variations** I, II, III, V

him since 1943, when he made his first attempt at it, with Pollock, for an exhibition with Peggy Guggenheim: 'Collage somehow became my joy, and has been ever since. Also, it has another function: Sometimes I get stuck in painting … and often, after shifting to collage for a time, I may resolve the painting problem when I return to it.'[9] But collage had its difficulties too.

The problem is, given these disparate and conflicting elements, how ultimately to unify *them. It's a painful and precarious way of making order. The separate elements tend to carry on guerrilla warfare with each other, a source of tension, true, but also possibly of chaos.*

Nevertheless Motherwell rated collage methods highly: 'I think for a long time I was the only or almost the only American artist who was not solely a collage-maker who consistently took it very seriously'.[10] Motherwell's collage prints, such as the *America-La France Variations* series of 1983–84 (named after the company that made American fire engines, rather than being the artist's salute to the culture of France) reveals the multiple changes each image underwent over time. The nine prints and multiple progressive proofs attest the painstaking process he undertook.

One of the unique characteristics of printing is that, after all the creative struggle, conflicts, revisions, starts and restarts that go into the process of trying to make a human expression as equivalent as possible to states of being — all that is buried in the working proofs.[11]

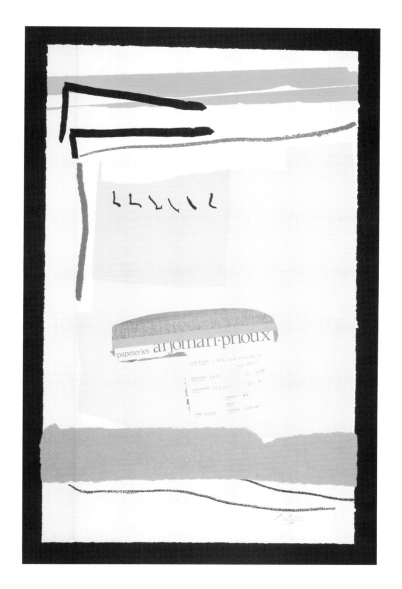

Motherwell proceeded back and forth with the collages, adding, subtracting, altering and sometimes almost beginning again. The process of collage making and proofing was exploratory, the artist seeking the perfect resolution. In her analysis of this body of work, Pat Gilmour has noted that these prints 'reveal the procedure used in many of the others'; they also 'bear testimony not only to Tyler's prodigious energy, but to his phenomenal patience'.[12]

A FOREIGN COUNTRY

Helen Frankenthaler and Motherwell were the exceptions in Abstract Expressionist circles, in that they became involved in printmaking. Motherwell made his first lithographs at ULAE from 1961 to 1963, having been encouraged to work there by Frankenthaler, his wife.

The indefatigable Tatyana Grosman played her role in encouraging him, but he was evasive when she described the beauty of a lithographic stone, and responded that there were other beautiful things, such as women or cars. When he did attend the ULAE workshop, he found the ambience and Grosman's European discretion appealing.

In his Gemini GEL days, Ken Tyler had also been keen to work with Robert Motherwell.

Bob was on my shopping list for some time, but I always knew until he left Marlborough Galleries I wouldn't stand a chance. They had an exclusive on both his paintings and his prints for almost ten years. When I heard that he went to M. Knoedler in 1972, I quickly flew to Provincetown, Massachusetts [where Motherwell lived] and saw him.

Motherwell enjoyed the camaraderie of the workshop, in contrast to the solitude of the studio where he had to confront an empty canvas and was solely reliant on his own resources. But he also found working in a big workshop system daunting, likening the experience to moving from playing the piano in the privacy of your home and enjoying the experience, to playing before an audience of 3,000 who wait to watch you being inspired. He found that such a set-up placed great strains on his creativity.

What actually happens when you're going to work with a noted printer/publisher such as Tamarind or Gemini or Tyler or Universal Limited Art Editions is that you arrive, say, at ten o'clock and are introduced to everybody. There are five or six printers standing around, there are a couple of secretaries, there's usually a photographer — maybe a member of the staff — and, in effect, you realize with a sinking heart that an enormous amount of time and money and organization has been set aside in a definite time slot for you to be a creative genius. Now there's no situation that freezes your blood more.[15]

Although born in California, Motherwell once remarked that returning there from the east coast seemed like being in a foreign country, because the culture was so different, and he found working in Los Angeles an alien experience. However, his love of the physical characteristics of California — the landscape, the colours, the light — remained with him always.

WHAT'S ON HIS MIND

When Tyler moved to the east coast in 1974, it was at Motherwell's suggestion that he eventually located the Tyler Workshop Ltd in the Bedford area, four miles away from the artist's home in Banksville, Connecticut. Their method of working together was unusual. Tyler has remarked that 'the biggest thing about Bob in a collaborative relationship and particularly mine with him … is that he comes from a position of great knowledge of the history of art.'

He has in his mind images from all mankind, not just from one school of painting, or one school of printmaking or one school of drawing. You don't really get to talking about Picasso or Johns or Kandinsky and how they made prints or are making prints. You're really involved in what Bob has to

We hit it off and he decided to come in March 1973 to do a project with me.[13]

Motherwell made a series of collages, 11 of which became the maquettes for a series of colour lithographs with collage, the *Summer Light* series, which was printed over a period of 12 months from September 1972. Eager to assist, Tyler organised a French papermaker, George Duchene, to develop for the series 'special cream handmade papers with RM as a watermark named Hawthorne of Larroque'.[14]

Robert MOTHERWELL
(above) **Bastos** 1974–75 colour lithograph
(opposite) **St Michael III** 1979 colour lithograph, screenprint

*say as a painter. The technique and all the 'cooking' …
doesn't matter to him … It's really more about what Bob's
been working on, what's on his mind … There isn't the
foggiest idea of how it's going to be technically — whether it's
going to be a single color print or a ten-color print, whether
it's going to be as you see it on the floor in the drawing stage,
or later with other things collaged on top; that's exciting,
because it's printmaking without any kind of program.*[16]

Motherwell was not interested in the printmaking
'recipes', the production and the process. In this, Tyler
likens him to Albers, 'who used to say the "cooking" was
the damnation of the imagination'.

*It was an interesting way of telling someone he should stop
'cooking' and start thinking. Bob does a lot of thinking …
There are other artists who come into the studio and do fifty
times more work in the same amount of time.*[17]

Motherwell once described Tyler as a one-man search and
rescue squad, someone of extraordinary capabilities and
boundless energy — but Tyler would occasionally find the
process of their working together a little frustrating.

*You're there, your sleeves are rolled up, there's this work to be
done, you want to take the stone off, put it on the press,
and get to work. And you can't. You can't just walk away
either. You've got your hyperkinetic body running overtime,
and you're trying to look very calm and relaxed. And once in
a while he'll look over and say 'I know, you want this stone.
Go do something. Leave me alone'.*[18]

Initially, Motherwell wanted to work on a stone and in
black. This left him free to work without the assistance of
the printer, except for the actual printing — but that
would change. The workshop environment didn't suit
him, as Tyler recalls:

*Somewhere along the line Motherwell and I decided that it
was best for our collaboration if he worked on Sundays.
A good time for him aesthetically, a quiet time. He didn't like
a collaborative effort in a noisy workshop. He liked visiting
the shop, but he didn't like doing his drawing in the shop
with everyone around. He liked the studio on the weekends
and he liked to just get at it for a while before he worked.*[19]

During those Sundays Tyler and Motherwell's friendship
grew, and their working method evolved to suit the
needs of the artist. He would take his proofs home and
assess them quietly among his other work. After
contemplation and absorption of what he had done,
he was able to decide what worked and what didn't —
what was a real Motherwell.

Tyler was keen for Motherwell to work on a large scale,
but the artist continued making small prints. He was
a chain smoker and made use of cigarette boxes for his
collages, just as they appeared in the French Cubists'
works on café life. To encourage the him to think about
a larger scale, Tyler took one of the cigarette collages,
enlarged it and printed it. The exercise worked and
Motherwell incorporated this in a large collage print.
Editioned prints of *Bastos* of 1974–75 and the *St Michael*
series of 1975–79 ensued, which combined the torn
cigarette box elements with gestural sweeps in a powerful
and dramatic large-scale form.

de la noche de
España

In 1980 the *Motherwell* retrospective exhibition was held at the Centro Cultural de la Caixa de Pensions, Barcelona, which then travelled to the Fundaçion Juan March, in Madrid. While Motherwell was in Spain for the exhibition, the poet Rafael Alberti read a poem dedicated to one of the prints in Mothwewell's *Elegies to the Spanish Republic* series. Motherwell returned to America with the poem and a desire to make an artist's book. He was discouraged by the limitation of the uniform sizes of the pages. Tyler suggested making a book with pages of different sizes that would complement the imagery. The solution was to have three page sizes which would fold out, and this formed the structure of *El Negro* of 1983, with the accompanying poem, *El Negro Motherwell*, by Alberti.

Robert Motherwell *El Negro* with the poem *El Negro Motherwell* by **Rafael Alberti,** Bedford Village, New York: Tyler Graphics Ltd, 1983 colour lithography, letterpress in a case covered in natural buckram cloth
(opposite top to bottom) *El Negro* 1983, pages 15–17, 47–49, 59–61
(above) boxed book (left) *El Negro* 1983, page 65

For Motherwell: *Lithography is a chameleon. You can make a lithograph as complicated as a French 19th-century academic painting. But its fundamental nature is limestone, a unique quality which Daumier perhaps understood best. Great lithography has to do with the stoneness of stone.*[20]

The artist's simple, subtle and powerful approach to the technique is evident in his body of lithographs, and particularly in the 'massive' use of black in *El Negro*. With this work he intended to evoke the feeling of Federico García Lorca's 'Lament for Ignacio Sánchez Mejias', which has a resonance far beyond an elegy for the dead matador to become a metaphor for the tragedy of the Spanish Civil War.

Black was the most resonant of colours: *I belong — I suppose to the degree than I can tell — to a family of 'black' painters and earth-color painters in masses, which would include Manet and Goya and Matisse ... There are certain works of Picasso that belong to that family too; Miró certainly.*[21]

TURNING TO MEDITERRANEAN LIGHT
Motherwell remained wary of becoming infatuated with colour. Rarely did he venture away from the pigments of the earth and light.

My iconography can cope with ... the blueness of blues, light and air and color, walls, perspective, and a general sense of the Mediterranean; with solitude, weight, intensities, placing, decisiveness, and ambiguities.[22]

Towards the end of his life, after years of working with Tyler, Motherwell's reluctance to use other colours diminished, particularly after Tyler moved to the purpose-built Mount Kisco workshop, with its on-site paper mill. This state of the art building was designed by the architect Michael Forstl, and Tyler Graphics Ltd was launched at its new address on 10 January 1987 with artists, including Motherwell, in attendance.

In these last years, Tyler observed that Motherwell, 'seemed to want to work in colour and we were extremely anxious for him to do that, so we kept adding colour to the black and whites … The paper mill started to have some magical influence on him.'[23] The final group of works Motherwell made with Tyler reflects this changing interest and the printer's keenness for this to happen. That group includes *Blue Elegy* 1987and *Mediterranean Light* of 1991, which combine lithography and colour pressed paper pulp, providing a richness and a saturation of colour not achieved before by this artist.

Motherwell's work at the Mount Kisco workshop became explorations of the scale and energy which, as a young man, he had foreseen as the future for American art; and a far cry from the rudimentary steps he took in the early 1940s.

Robert MOTHERWELL
(opposite) **Blue Elegy** 1987
colour relief, lithograph on TGL handmade, hand-coloured paper
(above) **Burning Elegy** 1991
colour lithograph, hand-coloured on TGL handmade, hand-coloured paper

Robert MOTHERWELL
Mediterranean Light 1991 colour lithograph on TGL handmade, hand-coloured paper

Notes
1. Robert Motherwell, in Barbaralee Diamonstein, 'An Interview with Robert Motherwell', in H.H. Arnason (ed.), *Robert Motherwell*, 2nd edn, New York: Harry N. Abrams, 1982, p. 229; for a more recent publication on the subject see Siri Engberg and Joan Banach, *Robert Motherwell: the complete prints 1940–1991, catalogue raisonné*, Minneapolis: Walker Art Center in association with Hudson Hills Press, New York, 2002.
2. 'A Special Genius: works on paper', *Bulletin of Rhode Island School of Design*, Winter 1977, pp. 20–34, quoted in Stephanie Terenzio, *The Prints of Robert Motherwell* (catalogue raisonné by Dorothy C. Belknap), New York: Hudson Hills Press, 1991, p. 24.
3. ibid., p. 38.
4. Stephanie Terenzio, *The Prints of Robert Motherwell* (catalogue raisonné by Dorothy C. Belknap), New York: Hudson Hills Press, 1991, p. 9.
5. Robert Motherwell, 'Animating Rhythm', in Stephanie Terenzio (ed.), *The Collected Writings of Robert Motherwell*, New York: Oxford University Press, 1992, p. 277.
6. Barbaralee Diamonstein, 'An Interview with Robert Motherwell', in H.H. Arnason (ed.), *Robert Motherwell*, 2nd edn, New York: Harry N. Abrams, 1982, p. 228.
7. ibid. pp. 229–231.

8. Stephanie Terenzio, *The Prints of Robert Motherwell* (catalogue raisonné by Dorothy C. Belknap), New York: Hudson Hills Press, 1991, pp. 84–85.

9. Barbaralee Diamonstein, 'An Interview with Robert Motherwell', in H.H. Arnason (ed.), *Robert Motherwell*, 2nd edn, New York: Harry N. Abrams, 1982, p. 230.

10. ibid., pp. 229–230.

11. *Robert Motherwell: prints 1977–79* (exhibition catalogue), New York: Brooke Alexander, 1979, p. 2, quoted in Stephanie Terenzio, *The Prints of Robert Motherwell* (catalogue raisonné by Dorothy C. Belknap), New York: Hudson Hills Press, 1991, p. 84.

12. Pat Gilmour provides a careful analysis of the steps Motherwell took in the production of this series in 'Robert Motherwell & The America-La France Variations', in *Innovation in Collaborative Printmaking: Kenneth Tyler 1963–1992* (exhibition catalogue), Tokyo: the Yomiuri Shimbun and the Japan Association of Art Museums, 1992, p. 184.

13. Ken Tyler, correspondence with Jane Kinsman, 25 June 2002.

14. ibid.

15. Interview with S. Terenzio, 28 December 1979, quoted in Stephanie Terenzio, *The Prints of Robert Motherwell* (catalogue raisonné by Dorothy C. Belknap), New York: Hudson Hills Press, 1991, p. 128.

16. Stephanie Terenzio, *The Prints of Robert Motherwell* (catalogue raisonné by Dorothy C. Belknap), New York: Hudson Hills Press, 1991, pp. 81–84.

17. Stephanie Terenzio, *The Prints of Robert Motherwell* (catalogue raisonné by Dorothy C. Belknap), New York: Hudson Hills Press, 1991, p. 84.

18. ibid., p. 90.

19. Ken Tyler, Qantas Birthday Lecture, 14 October 1999, National Gallery of Australia, Canberra.

20. Robert Motherwell in Heidi Colsman-Freyberger, 'Robert Motherwell: words and images', *The Print Collector's Newsletter*, IV(6), pp. 125–129, quoted in Stephanie Terenzio, *The Prints of Robert Motherwell* (catalogue raisonné by Dorothy C. Belknap), New York: Hudson Hills Press, 1991, p. 89.

21. Barbaralee Diamonstein, 'An Interview with Robert Motherwell', in H.H. Arnason (ed.), *Robert Motherwell*, 2nd edn, New York: Harry N. Abrams, 1982, p. 231.

22. *Robert Motherwell's A la Pintura: the genesis of a book* (exhibition catalogue), New York: Metropolitan Museum of Art, 1972, quoted in Stephanie Terenzio, *The Prints of Robert Motherwell* (catalogue raisonné by Dorothy C. Belknap), New York: Hudson Hills Press, 1991, p. 65.

23. Ken Tyler, Qantas Birthday Lecture, 14 October 1999, National Gallery of Australia, Canberra.

94

A Matter of Translation
Helen Frankenthaler

An artist who has made extraordinary prints at both the Bedford Village and Mount Kisco workshops is Helen Frankenthaler. In the early years of Gemini GEL, Tyler had been as keen to make prints with Frankenthaler as he had been to work with Motherwell. Prior to that time, she had made an innovative body of prints, principally at ULAE where she produced lithographic compositions in brush and wash, as well as colour woodcuts. She began working at ULAE in 1961 after finally succumbing to Tatyana Grosman's many invitations. Frankenthaler arrived at the workshop with virtually no technical knowledge: 'The whole idea of translating black tusche proofs into eventual colour was new to me.'[1]

For this established painter, the transition from her painting practice to printmaking was difficult: 'I had to work out a way … of being completely myself, the way I am working alone on a painting. The idea grows from the painting; you also bring an idea to it, and you often have to act at once, and then to stand back.' While in the print workshop:

If somebody said, 'We'll, do it, but it won't work. You can't throw a pail of tusche on a stone and use a tissue or your fingers or undistilled water or then take a tusche stick and scribble inside that pool of watery tusche', I felt, 'Why not? What's going to happen?' [2]

Frankenthaler ultimately fell out with Grosman, and legal proceedings over disbursement of proofs followed. Motherwell also had problems with proofs at ULAE although, according to Tyler, he 'was most generous during the proof split sessions. He understood the need for publisher archives and the importance of them going to museums.'[3]

FLOATING FORMS

Frankenthaler was an abstract artist from the beginning. She had initially studied at Dalton School, New York, and Benington College, Vermont (under the artist Hans Hofmann), then attended postgraduate classes in fine arts in 1949 at Columbia University, where one of her teachers was Meyer Schapiro, who also supervised Motherwell. With her first solo exhibition of paintings at New York's Tibor de Nagy Gallery in 1951 under her belt, she came to prominence the following year, when she astonished the art world with her *Mountains and Sea* of 1952. This painting reveals both her debt to Jackson Pollock — from whom she learned to paint instinctively and from all four sides of the canvas — and her own lyrical style.

Frankenthaler developed a reputation for producing extraordinary, evocative, abstract landscape paintings of washes, achieved by staining an unprimed canvas with diluted oil paint. An example is *Other Generations* of 1957, with its open composition and delicate gestural forms. Later compositions in synthetic polymer paint, including *Hillside* and *Java* of 1971, continue this way of painting. The significance of Frankenthaler's art has previously been overlooked, and her painting sometimes dismissed as too poetic and not sufficiently 'heroic' compared to the work of her fellow Abstract Expressionists. When her then partner, the art writer and critic Clement Greenberg, ushered the young Color Field artists, Morris Louis and Kenneth Noland, into her studio to see *Mountains and Sea*, they were both inspired. Yet her inventive, experimental style has been accorded less recognition than the work of the artists she influenced.

(opposite) **Helen FRANKENTHALER Other Generations** 1957 oil on canvas

Although Tyler had made overtures to Frankenthaler in the mid-60s, she declined the invitation to work with him 'due to her relationship with ULAE'. On her visits to Los Angeles from her home on the east coast in the early 1970s, Tyler tried again: 'I invited her to see the workshop on one of her visits and have lunch.' She accepted his invitation for lunch in 1972 and, during this encounter 'she expressed her negative feelings for the workshop'. Indefatigable, Tyler continued to pursue her after he moved his workshop to the east coast: 'I kept sending her brochures of my productions once I set up in Bedford.'⁴

Tyler's move to Bedford Village, the workshop's close proximity to Frankenthaler's home, and the artist's split with ULAE, were all factors that made her amenable to working with Tyler. But because of the sensitivities of her divorce from Motherwell (they had married in 1958 and divorced in 1971), Tyler first asked Motherwell if he would mind if Frankenthaler came to work at Tyler Graphics Ltd. He recalls:

Finally, in 1976 we did start to collaborate on her first three litho prints with TGL, Harvest, Dream Walk and Barcelona

… Helen did, however, like what Bob was doing with me and this was probably the reason that she was serious about working with me in 1976.[5]

These first lithographs made with Tyler are a product of perfect registration, in which multiple stones and aluminium plates achieved Frankenthaler's desired floating forms with apparent effortlessness. By the time she came to work at Tyler Graphics Ltd, the artist had become a thoroughly accomplished printmaker with a substantial body of graphic work. *Tiger's Eye* of 1987,

produced at the Mount Kisco workshop, combines lithographic washes with aquatint, etching and screenprinting. For this print, Frankenthaler used the mylar lithographic technique Tyler introduced had introduced to Hockney for his *Moving Focus* series.

Helen FRANKENTHALER
(opposite) **Tiger's Eye** colour trial proof I/3 1987 colour aquatint, lithograph, etching, screenprint
(above) **Tiger's Eye** 1987 colour aquatint, lithograph, etching, screenprint

97

RAVISHING SURFACES

The idea for Frankenthaler's masterpiece *Gateway Screen* took many years to evolve. In 1982 she had begun work on a colour intaglio and relief print on three sheets, *Gateway*, which was editioned in 1988. She was not completely satisfied with its planned folded print format. At that time, Ken Tyler was involved in making screens, having completed both Hockney's *Caribbean Tea Time* of 1987 and Steven Sorman's *From Away* of 1988, and the team in the workshop at Mount Kisco had some experience in this field. Frankenthaler, too, had been engaged by the idea of the screen, particularly since seeing the exhibition *The Folding Image: Screens by Western Artists of the 19th and 20th Centuries* at the National Gallery of Art, Washington in 1984.

At the time of making the *Gateway* prints, Tyler and Frank Stella had been working with the Tallix Foundry in Beacon, New York, not far from the Mount Kisco workshop. Tyler suggested to Frankenthaler that they make a cast bronze screen, and the project evolved from that point. 'Helen Frankenthaler's screen was something that kind of came in through the back door', according to Tyler.

It first was a three-panel intaglio print that she thought was really quite lovely as a folded print. But that didn't work too well on the wall, so we then moved into thinking about doing it as a screen. And at that time, doing a lot of foundry work and being around Frank Stella for a long time, it seemed to me that we could use the foundry that he was working at ... So we took Helen Frankenthaler down there one day and showed it to her and said, 'Perhaps you could do a bronze frame and then we would cast it and we would mount the print in there and we would have the screen in.'[6]

Helen FRANKENTHALER Gateway (screen) trial proof II 1988 hand-patinated cast bronze screen in three panels (verso)

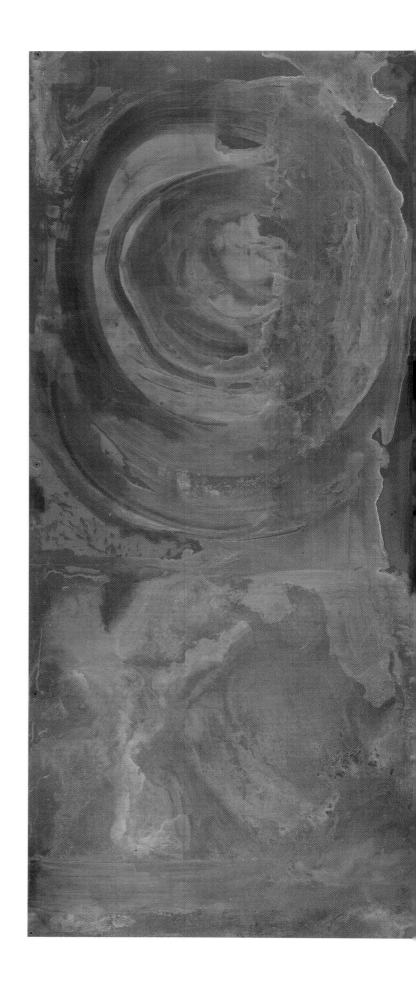

99

Working with the lost-wax casting process, to produce parts of the frame of the editioned version of the screen, appealed to Frankenthaler. At the suggestion of the owner of the foundry, she used sand-blasted bronze plates, which formed the back of the screen. These she painted individually with acids, to produce ravishing bronze surfaces with patinas of extraordinary beauty. The editioned intaglio print, *Gateway*, was placed on the front of the screen. In all of Frankenthaler's work with Tyler this was a unique collaboration.

I never thought that I could take an artist with the personality of Helen Frankenthaler and put her into a foundry, but she worked very well and undertook many repeat visits. But I don't think we will ever get her back into the foundry. It is a pretty laborious thing.[7]

EASTERN ROMANCE

Perhaps Frankenthaler's most inventive prints are those made with woodblocks. Her ability with this medium was quite apparent by the time she made jigsaw prints at ULAE. This method of printmaking had been used to great effect by Paul Gauguin and Edvard Munch to achieve bold expressionist works at the turn of the nineteenth century. In this process a single piece of wood is cut to form the separate elements of the composition, which are inked and, put back together and then printed. Frankenthaler found it 'the most freewheeling, fluid tool for getting into a woodcut, more than grooving with a knife into a wood surface or shading with splinter strokes'.[8] She was to make the jigsaw woodcut fully a part of her twentieth-century printmaking.

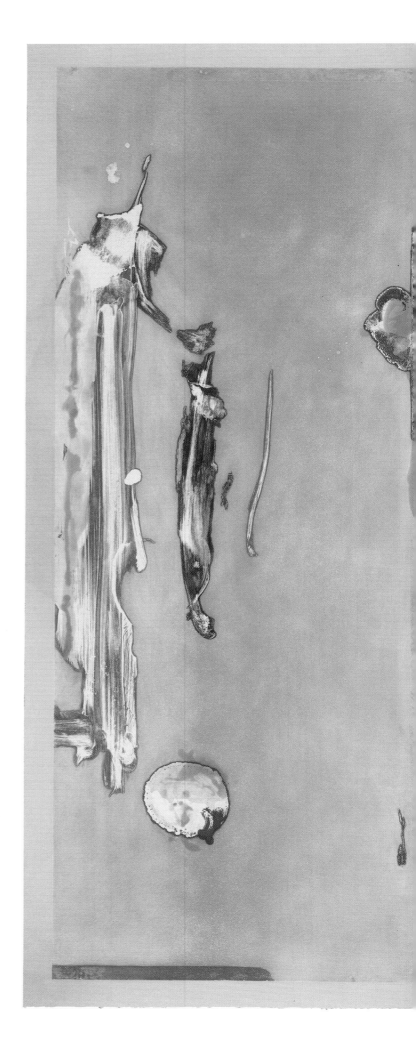

Helen FRANKENTHALER
Gateway (screen) 1988 colour etching, relief, aquatint, stencil on three sheets (recto)

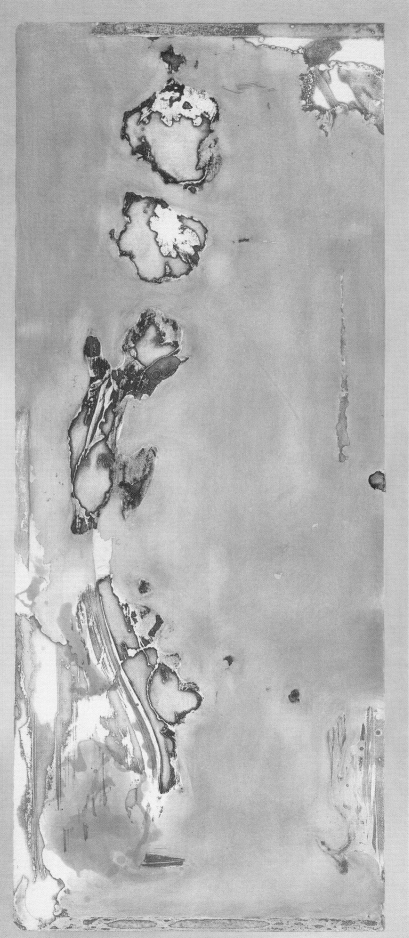

Frankenthaler has made other forms of woodcut and many of those made with Tyler are notable for their wash-like effects. The first of these, *Essence Mulberry* of 1977, took its title from the mulberry tree at the Bedford workshop that inspired the mellow dark reds of the print. The layering — almost floating — of colour and texture was achieved by selecting four from an original six blocks of wood: oak veneer for the yellow and brown, birch for the red, walnut for the blue and, Lauan plywood for the pink and dark blue. The combinations of these blocks, printed in perfect registration, recall the appealing faded quality of the exhibits in *Fifteenth-Century Woodcuts and Other Relief Prints in the Collection of the Metropolitan Museum of Art*, an exhibition Frankenthaler had seen that year in New York.

The paper selected for *Essence Mulberry*, handmade buff Maniai gampi, added an eastern romantic feel to this most delicate of works. The result was a work of evanescent beauty, using a woodcut technique that has frequently been employed for its blunt and brutal effects — by some of the early twentieth-century Expressionists and the Neo-Expressionists of the 1980s, for example.

Helen FRANKENTHALER
(left) **Essence Mulberry** 1977 colour woodcut on buff Maniai Gampi handmade paper
(opposite) **Cameo** 1980 colour woodcut on grey-pink TGL handmade paper

TRIAL AND ERROR

Tyler's collaboration with this demanding artist was at its closest and most radical during the making of the *Tales of Genji* series of prints. By this stage in her career, in the 1990s, Frankenthaler was keen to translate to printmaking the spontaneity and gestural qualities of painting. And it was a particular challenge for Tyler to offer the consummate printmaker something new in the field of the woodcut. He suggested that she begin by painting some carefully selected woods, and provided her with a range of brushes and sponges to experiment with. After painting several panels, she chose six exquisite examples which became the studies for this series of prints. What to do next? Frankenthaler was open to suggestion, perhaps unusually so. True to form, Tyler had an idea.

We should try something based on what we have already been experimenting with, the ukiyo-e principle of printing, but let's kind of throw away the washi paper, and let's make our own handmade paper. And let's not use a baren to rub through the back side onto the block, but use hydraulic presses. And let's see what Yasu and I can come up with in terms of making some blocks for you, and let's just keep this as free as possible.[9]

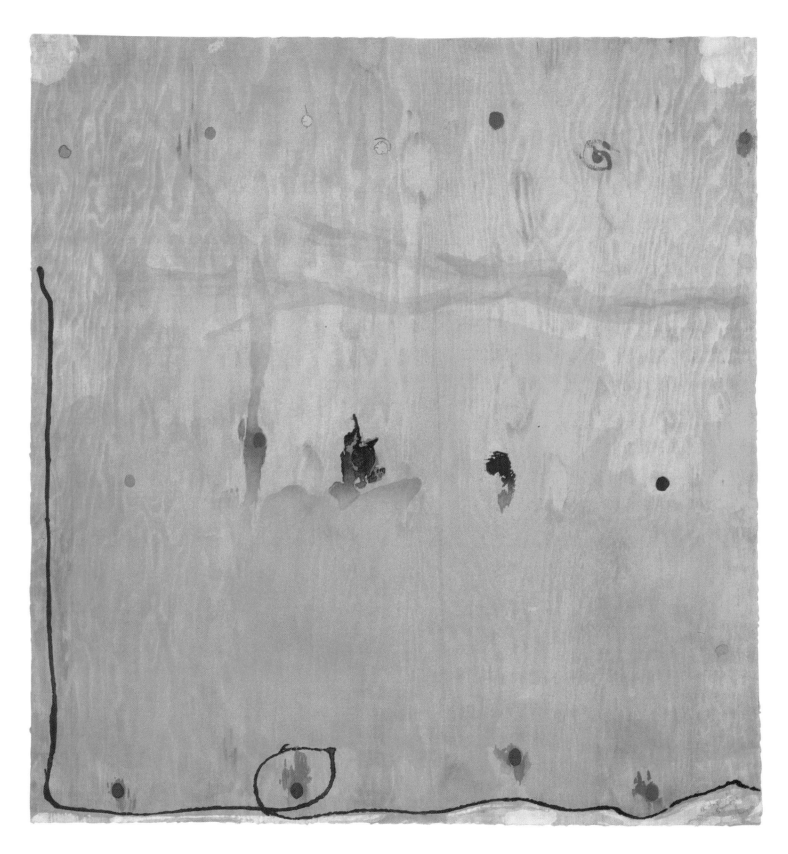

Helen FRANKENTHALER
(opposite) **Tales of Genji I** 1998 colour woodcut on light sienna
TGL handmade paper
(above) **Tales of Genji II** 1998 colour woodcut on pale orange
TGL handmade paper

Working with Tyler at that time was Yasuyuki Shibata, a Japanese printer versed in the art of ukiyo-e. He came to Bedford to work on woodcuts and to introduce this Japanese traditional art form to the workshop.

Helen FRANKENTHALER
(above) **Tales of Genji III** 1998 colour woodcut, stencil on grey
TGL handmade paper
(opposite) **Tales of Genji IV** 1998 colour woodcut, stencil on light rose
TGL handmade paper

Tyler was keen to know what could be done to push the medium further. Tom Strianese experimented with making special papers to replicate the grainy look of the painted wood panels. Frankenthaler spent many hours proofing, over and over again to achieve the desired results.

Tyler recalls Frankenthaler's practice: *She was very used to tickling the surface whether it be a stone or a metal plate, Frankenthaler endlessly tickles it until every little nuance that she is craving is absolutely accomplished. She loves to proof, for a long time. If you allow Helen she will proof for the rest of her life and never give you an edition.*[10]

Experimentation and proofing continued, and the artist became increasingly captivated by the process. It was a 'trial and error' method in which Frankenthaler gave the workshop team the latitude to do what was required. They tried a new system, using one surface block and one relief carved block on dyed papers. The resulting prints have a wonderful painterly quality about them. The use of the hydraulic press to squeeze the water from the pigment allowed for beautiful washes of colour and bleeding of forms not usually associated with the woodblock technique. Colours were both vibrant and evanescent. These prints were several years in the making, with the artist visiting the workshop many times, but the *Tales of Genji* are exceptional as testimony to great creativity and the potential of collaboration.

Helen FRANKENTHALER
(opposite) **Tales of Genji V** 1998 colour woodcut, stencil on rust
TGL handmade paper
(above) **Tales of Genji VI** 1998 colour woodcut, stencil on tan
TGL handmade paper

Helen Frankenthaler painting on a wood panel for
Tales of Genji III, Tyler Graphics Ltd artist's studio, 1995
(photograph Marabeth Cohen-Tyler)

NOTES ON
Tales of Genji

Kenneth E. Tyler [1]

With her latest prints, TALES OF GENJI I–VI, Helen Frankenthaler returns to one of the oldest forms of printmaking, woodcut, and infuses the medium with renewed intensity. Appropriately for the series title, the artist chose a romance about the passionate meanderings of an emperor's son in Heian Japan, a unique tribute to what many consider to be the world's first novel. *The Tales of Genji*, written by a court lady known as Murasaki Shikibu in the 11th century, has inspired innumerable *ukiyo-e*[1] woodcuts since it was written. However, these new prints have distinctly stepped outside the *ukiyo-e* tradition and beyond what Frankenthaler has already achieved in her past woodblock editions.

Her early woodcuts, *East and Beyond* (1973), *Essence Mulberry* (1977), *Cameo* (1980) and *Freefall* (1993) have been referred to as some of her finest printmaking efforts. For these, Helen often began by finding the right piece of wood, one which offered a grain that spoke to her aesthetically. The proofing session would begin by having the wood inked and printed onto carefully selected papers to study the character of the grain. Then she would draw out various shapes and continue to cut or mark the wood surface until her images emerged. She used carving instruments of all sizes and shapes, the jigsaw and power tools. Eventually her worked blocks were proofed in color and reworked to yield the texture and color nuance she sought. As more woodblocks were added for additional color the same process was often repeated.

Having mastered the techniques for making these prints, by 1995 Helen was anxious to extend her graphic abilities and embark on a project that would challenge both her own knowledge and that of the workshop. The artisans at Tyler Graphics were already involved in printing her first book, *This Is Not A Book*[2], and the creative atmosphere

was high. It was a good time for the artist and workshop to begin another graphic journey!

Collaboration on this project has been an exciting and rewarding experience for all involved. It was apparent from the beginning that what was needed was a new approach and technique for making what Helen strove for: a woodcut with painterly resonance. Knowing how important a painted model can be in helping solve this, I gave her a selection of six wood panels to paint on. She studied each for its grain and overall texture before she proceeded to stain and paint them. The results were six lush paintings on wood. We had our approach — we then needed to develop a special means for translating these exceptional paintings into prints, bringing out the expressive qualities of the wood panels. We mutually decided that it would be wonderful to make color handmade paper to match the different tones of the six wood panels and proceed from there. John Hutcheson and Tom Strianese quickly produced an assortment of colored papers for proofing. Helen and I reviewed her past woodcut editions and discussed how it might be possible to create a *ukiyo-e* style print on our large cotton papers. It was decided that our woodcut printer, Yasuyuki Shibata and I would start experimenting with this direction in mind. Helen made a *ukiyo-e* print[3] in Kyoto in 1983 and was familiar with the technique, which left her with positive and negative feelings about the process. During our conversations, it became apparent that the three of us (Helen, Yasu and I) would have to alter the technology and open up the medium for greater flexibility if we were to succeed with this project.

Since the goal was to make a woodcut with watercolor effects, we employed a hydraulic press to squeeze the inked blocks into the thick and absorbent cotton handmade paper, purposefully causing certain colors to bleed. For printing, Yasu created a combination of carved and textured blocks of his own invention. Helen's catchwords in directing the carving were liquidity, muzziness, painterly nuance, and perfectly registered color passages. These adjectives and phrases echoed in our heads as Yasu and I mapped out the many blocks and colors needed for Helen to make the woodcuts using the painted panels as models. It was clear from the beginning that this project would be experimental, often unpredictable, and painstakingly slow to carve, proof and edition. This would have made the project nearly impossible to do had it not been for Helen's sympathetic and encouraging support.

Before each print began, John and Tom would make the color paper to match the tonality of the painted-panel model, a process that required countless days making color batches of paper before the correct color was approved by the artist. Yasu would sample the papers for the proper amount of sizing[4] and thickness. Once approved, the edition of paper would be made and each sheet carefully calendered[5] to even out the surface. Yasu arranged an area in the main workshop for carving and we equipped a corner of the paper room for mixing inks, dampening the paper, sizing the paper and printing on the hydraulic press. As if he just arrived from the Edo period in a time warp, Yasu began to practise his uncanny skill as a carver and printer[6]. His inventiveness led to the development of textured blocks with sunken and abraded areas for printing colors without hard edges. Through many trial-and-error proofing sessions, we slowly developed techniques for bleeding the printed colors, and for embossing and imprinting wood grain and relief effects.

The constant wetting and blotting of the papers for printing each new color block resulted in a loss of color from previous printings. To counterbalance this occurrence, the papers were intermittently sized to help the watercolor adhere more securely to the papers during the wetting and blotting stages. The artist chose to have several of the last color runs stenciled to achieve stronger color saturation in selected passages. Assisted occasionally by Christopher Creyts who also studied woodblock printing in Japan, the project involved 90 woodblocks, 231 colors, and took nearly three years to complete — an accomplishment that is a tribute to Yasu's strength, stamina and creative understanding as a carver and printer.

Even with the exacting labor employed for the production of these works, Helen's images emerge as vigorous as *sumi* brushstrokes, masterfully applied without hesitation or constraint. In fact, the imagery has weightlessness — nothing is static and, with all the magical layers of thinly printed pigments, nothing is flat. It is a fitting tribute to the *ukiyo-e* legacy, since the word itself denotes the 'floating world', a reference to the flowering in the arts and freedom of expression which reigned from 1615 to 1868 in Edo, Japan. These are present-day *ukiyo-e* images, created by an American master, filled with abstract and poetic 'lightness' and luminosity. They were created by the artist in close collaboration with a team of dedicated craftspeople, artists in their own right.

Notes

1. *Ukiyo-e* (Japanese 'pictures of the floating world') The popular art of the 17th to the 19th Century which conjured up the life of the times. Geishas and Kabuki actors were favorite subjects, but *ukiyo-e* artists also depicted landscapes and scenes from historical epics, legends and folktales. Color woodcut prints were a major means of expression. The most famous artists of this period were Utamaro, Hokusai and Hiroshige.
2. *This Is Not A Book* is a *livre de luxe* consisting of nine colorful intaglios, two lithographs and seven pages of lithographed text, bound in half quarter calf leather and cloth. The book is in an edition of 50 plus proofs.
3. The traditional *ukiyo-e* print is printed by first placing the paper onto the face of the inked block and firmly rubbing from the back side of the paper with a baren. A baren is a circular disk of batting covered with flat bamboo sheathing twisted to form a grip. The tool is moved in a semi-circular direction using very firm downward pressure, requiring great arm and hand strength. Japanese traditional paper is *washi*; a paper made from plant fibres, primarily *kozo* fibre. This paper is strong enough to withstand the repeated pressure of the baren.
4. Sizing is an application of a synthetic material to the paper pulp to make the finished paper's surface more receptive to ink or watercolor. For this project, it was necessary for the printer to apply additional sizing materials during printing.
5. Calendering is the process of giving a smooth finish to paper by running it through either a press or a series of rolls which iron and polish it.
6. The practice during the Edo period was for a woodcut to be made by a team of craftsmen: papermakers, carvers, and printers. Each task requires unique skills and different groups of trained muscles, therefore it was difficult for one person to perform all of these tasks with equal efficiency. Today it is common for printers to perform all of these functions.

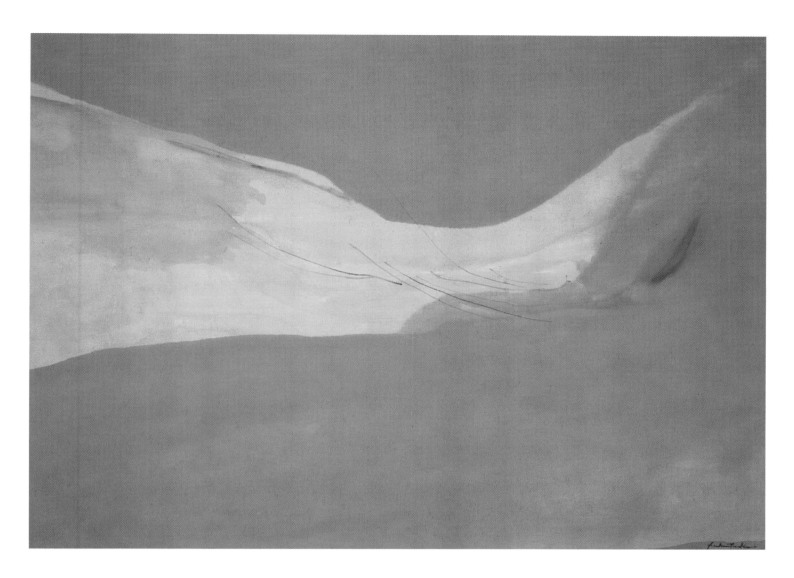

Helen FRANKENTHALER
Java 1971
synthetic polymer paint on canvas
Collection Museum of Contemporary Art, Sydney

In a discussion in the mid-1970s with Judith Goldman, Helen Frankenthaler spoke of her attitude to printmaking in the early years: 'I was a painter', she said, 'I didn't want to monkey around with acids, paper, travel. I worked on unsized, unprimed cotton duck and was not involved with precious editions or working small.'[12] Her printmaking, however, is the very antithesis of 'monkeying around' on a small scale. Frankenthaler's graphic art, particularly the most recent woodcuts made with Tyler, reveal her to be an accomplished and innovative artist, unafraid of scale and experimentation, while taking the art of the woodcut to a new level.

Notes
1. Helen Frankenthaler, quoted in Suzanne Boorsch, 'Conversations with Prints', in Pegram Harrison, *Frankenthaler: a catalogue raisonné, prints 1961–1994*, New York: Harry N. Abrams, 1996, p. 17. See also. Judith Goldman, 'Painting in Another Language', *ARTnews*, 74(7) September 1975, pp. 28–31
2. Helen Frankenthaler, quoted in Suzanne Boorsch, 'Conversations with Prints', in Pegram Harrison, *Frankenthaler: a catalogue raisonné, prints 1961–1994*, New York: Harry N. Abrams, 1996, p. 16.
3. Ken Tyler, correspondence with Jane Kinsman, 29 May 2002.
4. Ken Tyler, correspondence with Jane Kinsman, 25 June 2002.
5. ibid.
6. Ken Tyler, Qantas Birthday Lecture, 14 October 1999, National Gallery of Australia, Canberra.
7. ibid.
8. Helen Frankenthaler, 'The Romance of Learning a New Medium for an Artist', *Print Collector's Newsletter*, 8(3) July–August 1977, p. 67, quoted in Pegram Harrison, *Frankenthaler: a catalogue raisonné, prints 1961–1994*, New York: Harry N. Abrams, 1996, p. 178–181.
9. Ken Tyler, Qantas Birthday Lecture, 14 October 1999, National Gallery of Australia, Canberra.
10. ibid.
11. Ken Tyler, 'Notes on Tales of Genji', in Ken Tyler, *Helen Frankenthaler: Tales of Genji*, Mount Kisco, New York: Tyler Graphics Ltd, 1998.
12. Helen Frankenthaler, quoted in Judith Goldman, *Frankenthaler: the woodcuts*, New York: George Braziller Inc with Naples Museum of Art, Florida, 2002, p. 8.

A Print Epic

Frank Stella

The collaboration between the foremost American abstract artist, Frank Stella, and Ken Tyler was once dubbed as 'part brinkmanship, engineering, and sometimes theater'.[1] By the early 1980s, Stella's work with Tyler had taken printmaking into new realms of rich imagination and experimentation. Stella had become an artist who was as important for his printmaking as he was for his painting.

The artist made a name for himself early in his career. In 1959, at the age of 24, he came to the attention of the New York art world when four paintings from his *Black Paintings* series of 1958–60 were selected for the important exhibition *Sixteen Americans*, at the Museum of Modern Art (MoMA), New York. These paintings were thought to be profound. Reflecting on his career, Stella commented: 'my career is backwards, it should have ended up with these profound, severe paintings. [But]they weren't profound and severe, or they might have been profound but by accident … they were extremely childish.'[2] In the same year as the MoMA exhibition, the director, Alfred Barr, acquired for the museum Stella's painting *The Marriage of Reason and Squalor* of 1959. The following year, Stella was given his first solo exhibition at the Leo Castelli Gallery in New York.

Stella was initially captivated by Abstract Expressionism. He later commented in one of the series of Charles Eliot Norton lectures he gave at Harvard University in 1983–84 that his aspirations as a young practitioner 'had already been realised to a certain extent by postwar abstract expressionism',

but I sensed something in their work which worried me more than the stunning level of their accomplishment impressed me.

Frank STELLA
Flin Flon 1970 synthetic polymer and fluorescent paint on canvas

I sensed a hesitancy, a doubt of some vague dimension which made their work touching, but to me somehow too vulnerable.[3]

The style, as it was practised by the second wave of Abstract Expressionist artists, did not attract Stella who described their work as 'chaotic, academic, and mannered'.[4]

A REFINED ABSTRACTION

Stella came to seek something more in his art, moving on to a more refined abstraction: 'I was convinced that a completely independent abstract art, one that had really severed its roots from a representational bias for pictorial depiction, would be an improvement, and would preserve and defend the accomplishment of abstract expressionist painting.'[5] He found inspiration in the art of Wassily Kandinsky and Kasimir Malevich. 'If Kandinsky was filling up the landscape with pigment, Malevich was doing even greater damage to the figure inhabiting that landscape. First he flattened it like a pancake, and then with incredible dispatch he obliterated it.'[6] These two artists, with Piet Mondrian, have remained inspirational for Stella, who remarked in a recent interview: 'For me, the spiritual resides in Mondrian, Malevich and Kandinsky, they are my spiritual basis. I mean my complete belief and commitment and appreciation of their work allows me to go forward. I can take that as given and I believe in it.'[7]

Also important for the artist was German-born Hans Hofmann, who had lived in Paris as a young man before moving to the United States in 1930. Hofmann was a significant figure in the evolution of Abstract Expressionism in America, an influential teacher and a brilliant colourist, who liked to quote Cézanne's dictum: 'When color is richest, form is fullest.'[8]

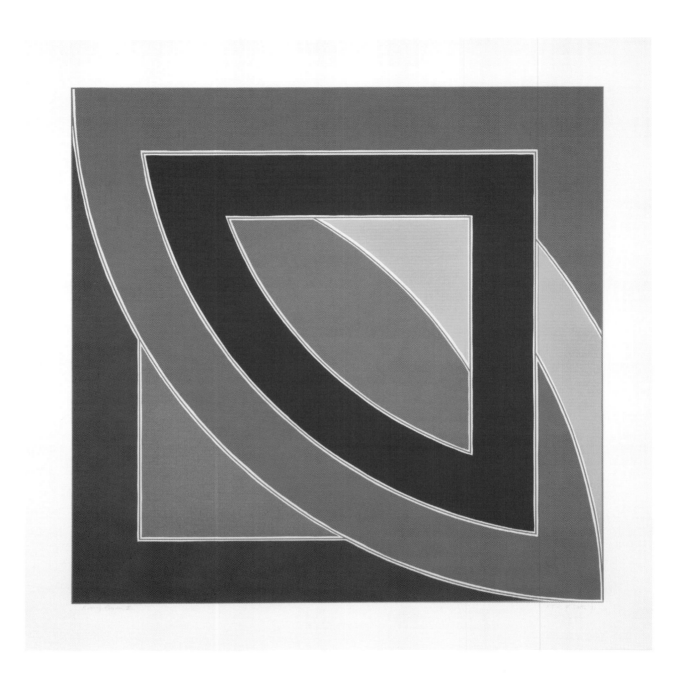

Stella was critical of Renaissance one-point perspective, where the image recedes from the picture plane, preferring space that appeared to move in and out of the canvas, both towards and away from the viewer. Vivid colour and inventive ways of dealing with space were also to become key characteristics of Stella's art.

The artist developed a thoroughly abstract style during the 1960s and 1970s, which focused on density of colour, symmetrical composition and an all-over design which destroyed illusionistic space. He chose to paint on a large scale with shaped canvases framing the forms of his compositions, so there would be no visual tricks.

Frank STELLA
(above) **River of Ponds I** 1971 colour lithograph
(opposite) **River of Ponds II** 1971 colour lithograph

'AND SOMETIMES THEATER'

In the early days of Gemini GEL, Stella was one of the artists Tyler cajoled into making prints at the workshop. During 1967, Tyler made many overtures to persuade the artist to work with him. Stella rejected Tyler's approaches initially, responding that he couldn't work by drawing with tusche because he only drew with felt-tipped pens. Tyler took this as a challenge and disguised lithographic tusche as ink in a marker pen — and Tyler's inventiveness 'seduced him'.[9] Although Stella remembers resisting, 'as hard as I could', he soon found himself 'chained' in the studio surrounded by aluminium plates and left to draw on them with lithographic crayon.[10] Thus began the collaboration of these two dynamic figures that has lasted 35 years — described by the art critic and author, Robert Hughes, as 'one of the great partnerships in modern American art'.[11]

At the beginning of the relationship, Stella's attitude to making prints was lukewarm.

I could only see it as a reproductive medium, as in making reproductions of images — you make a print of a painting … I could see prints for their own sake but they were sort of like drawings to me˙… I made some in the beginning, but they were basically about making drawings and reproducing those drawings as prints.[12]

Frank STELLA
(above) **River of Ponds III** 1971 colour lithograph
(opposite) **River of Ponds IV** 1971 colour lithograph

Stella's first print made with Tyler, therefore, was based on a drawing for a large-scale painting — planned but not executed. The painting was to have comprised six chevron-shaped canvases joined together, but the artist had not been able to find bolts of canvas big enough for the job, and the idea lapsed. The possibilities of printmaking were there: 'All he had to do was make a part'[13] — and that one chevron shape could be repeated again and again to produce the required form. The resulting *Star of Persia I* 1967 was Stella's first lithograph, printed perfectly and in the latest metallic inks.[14] This working method came to be one of the signature elements of Stella's creative process —

recycling imagery, and sustaining one art, be it painting, sculpture or print, by another. It became the heart of Stella's artistic development.

In 1967 Stella began a series of *Protractor* paintings, notable for their bold curvilinear forms, large scale and vivid colour. He developed a variant of these compositions which he enclosed in a square — such as *Flin Flon* of 1970. Painted in brilliant pigments in polymer and fluorescent paints, the symmetrical compositions and formal, organic shapes evoke Islamic pattern — something Stella was interested in at that time.

In the *Newfoundland* series of six prints Stella made at Gemini GEL in 1971, the composition was reworked in a less symmetrical format, with interlocking bold arcs and squares and vivid colouring. *River of Ponds I–IV*, from this group, are characterised by a complexity of dynamic forms and a resonant palette, which foreshadowed a new direction for the artist.

THE FROZEN GESTURE

Stella, with Tyler's assistance, developed a very direct way of making prints from inked metal reliefs collaged onto wood substrates. The result was the groundbreaking *Circuits* series from the first half of the 1980s, notable for their rich textures, flamboyant lines and suggestions of three-dimensionality. Stella recalled: 'It took quite a while for me to notice … that working with sculpture in a painterly way could yield a powerful printing tool.'[15]

During a sustained period of painting between 1981 and 1983, Stella produced the group of metal relief paintings, *Circuits*, whose curved forms suggest racing car speedways — car racing being a particular passion of the artist.

Frank STELLA
(above left and right) **Pergusa Three** 1982 colour trial proofs 4/5 and 5/5
colour relief, woodcuts on TGL handmade, hand-coloured paper
(opposite) **Pergusa Three** 1983 colour relief, woodcut on TGL handmade, hand-coloured paper

The brilliant colours and rich patterning were further embellished by etching of the surfaces; and with their forms layered in an inventive, sculptural version of the collage, these works stretched the boundaries of painting. Stella began this new approach with a degree of trepidation.

It seemed so industrial and it didn't make sense in painterly terms. What made it fall into place for me was the ability to change the surface. I didn't have to just paint on the surface but was able to etch into the surface. This was an idea that came obviously from printmaking.[16]

Until this point, Stella's painting continued to inform his printmaking. Then the reverse began to occur. While he was working with the Swan Laser Die Company in Bridgeport, Connecticut, where the metal honeycomb shapes were being cut for his *Circuits* relief paintings, he discovered a wonderful tracery of random lines on the plywood backing boards that had been pierced

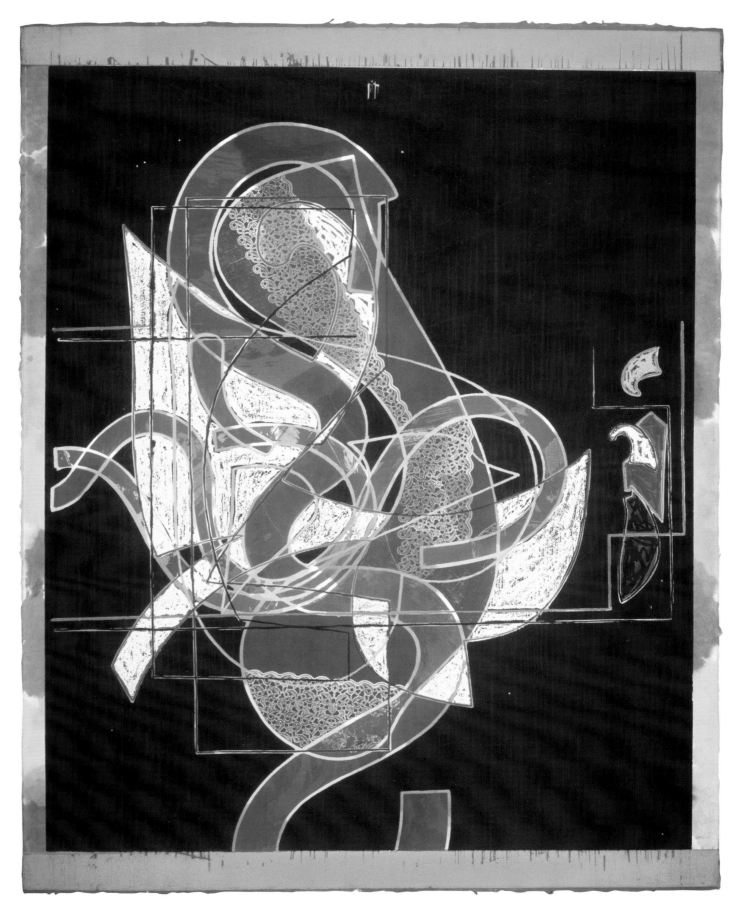

121

Frank STELLA
(opposite) **Pergusa Three Double** 1984 colour relief, screenprint, woodcut,
engraving on two sheets of TGL handmade, hand-coloured paper
(above) **Imola Three, State II** 1984 colour relief, woodcut on TGL handmade,
hand-coloured paper

by the laser cutting machine. It occurred to Stella that this board, with its tangled network of cut, curved lines, could be used as a printing element. No longer did his prints have to reproduce what he had done in painting; they could have their own language and style. 'I was struck by the beauty of the found drawing', wrote Stella of this experience.

It was amazingly fluid and complex, yet it seemed very natural, very unforced. It obviously reminded me of the webbed lines evoked by Pollock's paint skeins. At the same time, though, that I saw the configuration's connection to a painting, I also saw its obvious connection to printing. I suppose a negative imprint of Jasper's 0 through 9 must have popped into my mind. I loved the idea that simply inking the surface of the plywood board would produce

a web of white lines, if one only pressed a piece of paper against it. All of a sudden I had a way of working with printing that freed my hands, and I had a way of working with printing that could be developed alongside my work with painting.[17]

This discovery was to transform Stella's art. Evidence of it can be seen in the series *Circuits* of 1982–84, which were printed from a combination of etched magnesium plates and woodblocks. The prints were named after motor racing tracks, for example the *Imola* prints (after the course in Italy) and the *Pergusa* prints (after the Sicilian track). Their compositions hark back to Abstract Expressionism, particularly the art of Jackson Pollock. This revelatory period saw Stella produce an astonishing number of variants of his compositions, and his use of a combination of techniques added to that range.

The large scale of the works was to have an impact on the kinds of paper Stella used. In response to his need for larger paper sizes, the workshop developed its mill to be able to produce handmade paper as big as 168 x 132cm. Adding dyes to newly couched sheets of paper pulp — a technique that David Hockney and Helen Frankenthaler also used — was another innovation introduced to the artist by the Tyler studio.

Working with Tyler, Stella came to recognise how the print process could enhance his artistic concerns.

The power of the press, which grows mightier and mightier — especially when, as in Ken's case, it has to conform to ambitions of a supreme master printer — is that power that gives the visual punch to the stamped-out image of the print. This visual punch is a prized effect, because it is both optical and tactile, appealing to eyesight and touch as it brings color and surface, ink and paper together.[18]

The imaginative step from the very sculptural relief paintings, to printing elements to prints, was taken again into the third dimension with Stella's sculptures and the dome-shaped prints of his *Moby Dick Domes*.

MOBY DICK

Between 1985 and 1993, Stella produced a large group of works which take their titles from that great nineteenth-century literary classic, Herman Melville's *Moby-Dick*. They appear in the series *The Moby Dick Engravings* of 1991, *Moby Dick Domes* of 1992 and *Moby Dick Deckle Edges* of the following year. Stella also produced single prints with titles drawn from the chapter headings of Melville's epic novel, one being *The Fountain*.

The notion of a narrative was something that the artist had started to explore in earlier series, such as *Illustrations after El Lissitzky's Had Gadya* of 1982–84 — and he felt that the link to literary titles would make his abstractions more accessible. While reading Melville to his sons, Peter and Patrick, Stella found the prose pictorial in a way — 'the rhythms and everything are like the types of things that you can do using shapes ... a nice, kind of crisp, moving language'.[19]

Tyler recalls that Stella had decided very early on in the making of his Moby Dick imagery 'that each of the 135 chapters of the book would relate to a print, painting or sculpture ... the configuration dictating the choice of the title — what went with what'.[20] The prints, therefore, did not follow the sequence of the book, but were linked because of a synergy between word and image. As Stella noted: 'In general, the imagery and the activity is somewhat akin to what happens in the book, I mean, there's a lot of turbulence ... a lot of things happen, and there's a lot of movement, and the language is very colorful. So that's what these are about.'[21]

As the nexus between Stella's sculptural works and his prints grew, the notion of a sculptural print evolved.

The *Moby Dick Domes* are notable for their technical complexity and their excursion into the third dimension. Tyler later noted that Stella had 'taken to paper pulp in a very real way, using it in a very inventive way. He has helped us to move the print from its flat base to its sculptural base.'[22] After years of research to work out ways of making shaped paper, Tyler developed a vacuum method to produce the required sculptural form.

It is a vacuum system we had to invent and we also had to invent how to make the moulds ... It seemed that the dome series satisfied the need to break away from the flat surface and we haven't returned to it. Possibly because we know how long and difficult it was to get there.

If arriving at the shaped paper proved problematic, inking the shaped domes of the printing plates was an even more complex process.

Once we found out how we could transfer that imagery to this dish like shape we couldn't figure out how to keep the ink up on the sides, it kept running down into the centre. It took some time and we figured out all that and because we have all the kinds of presses that one needs to make multiple kinds of printings including hydraulic presses for the now considerable mould making experience. We were able to make moulds that could stamp the shaped paper into the shaped plates. And so what you really do have here is a very simple resolution. The background plate is flat and then the inside dome is the shaped plate. They are inked separately and brought together and put into the shaped mould, and the shaped paper is dropped on top of that, then a backing mould.[23]

Frank STELLA
(opposite) **Jonah Historically Regarded (Dome)**
colour etching, aquatint, relief, engraving, screenprint, stencil, handcoloured on shaped TGL handmade paper from the series *Moby Dick Domes* 1992

Frank STELLA
The Cabin: Ahab and Starbuck (Dome) colour etching,
aquatint, relief, engraving on shaped TGL handmade paper
from the series *Moby Dick Domes* 1992

126

AN EPIC PRINT

Sculptural prints were one avenue of exploration for Stella, mural prints were another. *The Fountain* of 1992 takes its title from chapter 85 of *Moby-Dick*, which describes in detail the majesty of the Sperm Whale — a beast of grand proportions which dominates the sea — and its wondrous breathing apparatus, which produces the spout that gave this episode its title.

In terms of scale and ambition, *The Fountain* is the most significant print of all the *Moby Dick* series. It should be viewed as Stella's magnum opus in printmaking to that point — a pivotal example of his abstract style, with signature forms, lines, colours, textures and layering, produced at a scale that reveals the gifts and confidence of the artist. It is one high point in Stella's collaboration with Tyler and represents the culmination of their working method, developed over some three decades. Stella and Tyler have refined the process of working from a completed collage, adopting a wide range of printing techniques for the one work, and editioning on specially made paper.

In their unique working method, 'Frank the scavenger,' as Tyler calls him,[24] creates the compositions from what the artist terms 'debris d'atelier' (studio debris), where past imagery, from Tyler's 'supply center', is recycled, and new imagery advanced — Tyler Graphics being the 'living inventory, a library of shapes and images' for Stella's art.[25]

From mid-1989, Stella worked on a collage, for the most part made from fragments of printed proofs 'using reject prints and partially printed proofs'.[26] The fragments, predominantly from *Moby Dick* prints, were collaged using a method of 'cutting up and stapling down'. Some fragments from past imagery were enlarged, some cut into new forms and some shapes reworked. As the process

of moving from collage to print took place over the years of the project, the design changed slightly, with certain variations in colour and the addition or subtraction of forms. Tyler has commented: 'He has some mapping system in his head that … [allows him to] keep all this together and be satisfied.'[27]

Once Stella had mapped out his imagery for *The Fountain*, Tyler and his team of assistants went to work behind closed doors in the studio to produce the image in its printable form — their magic, a result of phenomenal technical prowess and an unstoppable desire to break new ground. A few years after *The Fountain*, during the making of another print *Juam,* Tyler reflected on the process: 'When we know that we have come to some conclusion with that technique and we can repeat it, we'll open the door and say here, this is what we can do.'[28]

To translate *The Fountain* collage into print, it was decided to use both woodblocks and intaglio plates.

My choice of woodblock was made based on the large size of the print. Both Frank and I knew we were going to use some of the existing metal plates from the Moby Dick prints series. It was determined that the black image would be printed from the woodblock and the colors would be from metal insert plates.[29]

It was both the artist's and the printer's desire to use the most beautiful papers. In February 1990 Tyler got in touch with the Fuji Paper Mills Co-operative, Tokushima, 'to devil up large triple ply washi (kozo fibre)' on an enormous scale. The sheer bravura of the project can be seen in its scale, and for such a monumental undertaking a special 500-ton hydraulic platen press had to be designed.[30]

Frank STELLA
The Fountain 1992 colour woodcut, etching, aquatint, relief, drypoint, screenprint, collage, hand-coloured on 3 sheets of natural handmade, hand-coloured triple-layered kozo fibre and handmade natural gampi fibre

(opposite) Frank Stella observes as Kenneth Tyler and Yasuyuki Shibata position inked plates to print *The Fountain*, pressroom at Tyler Graphics Ltd, March 1992 (photograph Marabeth Cohen-Tyler)
(below) Three carved woodblocks for *The Fountain* (photograph Jim McHugh)

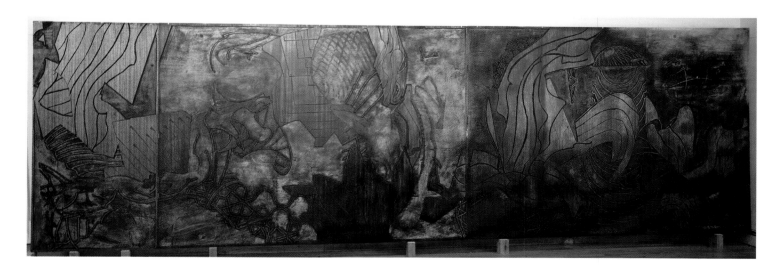

128

The Fountain is a 67-colour, hand-coloured woodcut, etching, aquatint, relief, drypoint, screenprint, on three sheets of natural kozo fibre handmade paper, with seven screenprinted natural gampi fibre handmade paper collage elements. Its spans 231.1cm in height by 700.4cm in length. It was derived from an original collage, and printed from three carved woodblocks and 105 intaglio plates.

This mural print is a masterpiece of abstraction, with an extraordinary group of shapes coalescing as a unified whole. It is a celebration of colour; lines are at once bold gestures or exquisitely delicate. In one work, Stella 'the mapper' and Tyler 'the magician' brought the art of printmaking to an extraordinary stage.

Frank STELLA from the series *Moby Dick Deckle Edges* 1993 colour lithographs, etching, aquatint, relief, engraving, screenprint on TGL handmade paper
(above) **Ambergris** trial proof V/12
(opposite) **Ambergris** trial proof XII/12

Ten years after *The Fountain* project began, Tyler recalled the remarkable nature of its evolution and of his collaboration with Stella. It was the principal work within the *Moby Dick* series, and the largest of the series, incorporating so much of Stella's imagery: 'It was a synchronised collaboration in all mediums coming together … the ideas flowed without hindrance … [a benefit of] all those rehearsals.' Tyler felt that the imagery itself told the story 'that the collaboration

was freer in *The Fountain* — there's a generosity in the image, there is nothing there of a struggle — we knew what we were there for'.[31]

In his series *Imaginary Places* of 1994–97, Stella continued to recycle and reinterpret his imagery while exploring new ways of composing, with the search as important as the result. The series combines many processes — lithography, screenprinting, etching, engraving, aquatint, relief, woodcut — all in glorious colour combinations that astonish with their boldness, and printed on beautiful handmade, dyed papers, sometimes in rectangular formats and sometimes in circular ones. For this series, Stella took the titles for the individual prints from *The Dictionary of Imaginary Places* by Alberto Manguel and Gianni Guadalupi (New York: Macmillan, *c.*1980).

Stella is an artist capable of working on many compositions at once, and he created a large body of work for the *Imaginary Places* series, committed to the search for perfection. *Juam* is one of two from the series of 1997 (the other being *Juam, State I)* that refer to another of Melville's novels, *Mardi*, originally published in 1849. Juam is a mythical island with rivulets, greenery and singing birds, and a magical palace, the House of Morning, which took five hundred moons to complete. Stella's magical and colourful imagery also took a long time to complete, because of an initial problem with a steel printing element that had to be replaced. The composition changed over time too, as Stella incorporated imagery recycled from the *Moby Dick* series.

Juam continues the further exploration of the third dimension in printmaking, with a rich sculptural quality derived from the method of its making. The printing elements for *Juam* consist of a carved plywood substrate with 102 irregularly shaped elements — one honeycomb aluminium; 39 copper and 12 magnesium plates; one bronze, 11 poured aluminium and 16 brass elements; and 22 aluminium rings. This collage of poured metal, of wonderfully irregular shapes and forms, was then inked with 144 colours, taking printmaking to yet another high point of excellence.

As with all projects at Tyler's studios since his early Gemini days, the printer's collaborative efforts with the artist relied on the orchestration of the various talents at the workshop. With *Juam*, for example, the Tyler Graphics documentation records that the handmade papers were made on site with Tom Strianese and Kevin Falco, and the preparation and processing of the aluminium lithographic plate was carried out by Kevin Falco and Christopher Creyts. Michael Mueller and assistants Nancy Bressler, Rolf Kaul and Falco worked on the screenprinting component. For the intaglio printing, magnesium plates were made by Swan Engraving and the copper plates were prepared and processed by Anthony Kirk. Stella prepared the woodblocks, assisted by Tyler. The task of assembling all the parts was carried out by Kirk, John Hutcheson, Tyler, Strianese, Falco, Creyts, and Todd Elkin. Finally *Juam* was proofed and editioned by Kirk, Hutcheson, Strianese, Brian Maxwell, Creyts, Bressler, Elkin and Kimberly Bursic.

This one work summarises so many of the Tyler workshops' great innovations — the use of handmade and dyed papers, multiple techniques and the large scale that has brought Frank Stella so far from the simply reproductive prints he first made with Ken Tyler in 1967.

Frank has established a vocabulary now that involves everything we do in the printmaking workshop. It is simply not enough to say that he has pushed us subtly day by day, as we have been working till the point where we are prepared for almost anything. And we are almost looking for it, and we have no idea where he is going to take us, but I am sure where he is going to take us will again improve our abilities and once again he will come up with something that is quite inventive. And perhaps ... even more compulsive than we have been in the past in our craft.[32]

During the making of *Juam* in 1997, Tyler mused: *I can't really say no to his ideas and he really can't stop having them and so, in a funny way, we're a good pair.*[33]

Frank STELLA
(opposite) Juam **Printing Matrix** 1997
(following pages left to right)
Juam 1997 colour relief, etching, aquatint, lithograph, screenprint, woodcut, engraving on two sheets of TGL handmade, hand-coloured paper
Juam, State I 1997 colour relief, woodcut, etching, aquatint, hand-coloured on two sheets of TGL handmade, hand-coloured paper

134

135

POSTSCRIPT

In 2001 Ken Tyler closed the Mount Kisco print workshop. The following year the National Gallery of Australia acquired a collection of more than 2,200 items by way of purchase and gift from Ken Tyler. This collection consists of editioned prints, screens and multiples, rare and unique proofs, and artists' drawings. Tyler also presented the Gallery with a generous gift of photographic records, film and audio material — historical primary source material recording artists' working methods from the 1960s to the present day.

The great donor to the National Gallery's International Prints, Drawings and Illustrated Books Department, the late Orde Poynton, AO, CMG, enthusiastically supported the proposal.

The collection now in Canberra encompasses a diverse range of the styles and working methods of some of the most significant contemporary artists working in America. Their work is a time capsule for present and future generations which chronicles phenomenal developments in postwar twentieth-century printmaking.

Anthony Kirk observes as Frank Stella assists in assembling inked and uninked plates before printing impressions of **Fanattia**, from *Imaginary Places,* 1994 (photograph Marabeth Cohen-Tyler)

136

Notes

1. Siri Engberg, 'Imaginary Places and the Art of the Everyday', in *Frank Stella at Tyler Graphics* (exhibition catalogue), Minneapolis: Walker Art Center, 1997, pp. 9–16.
2. Sidney Guberman, 'Frank Stella's Newest Prints — A Rage for Chaos', in *Frank Stella: Imaginary Places* (exhibition catalogue), Mount Kisco, New York: Tyler Graphics Ltd, 1995, pp. 3–11.
3. Frank Stella, *Working Space*, Cambridge, Mass.: Harvard University Press, 1986, p. 158.
4. Barbara Rose, *American Art since 1900*, rev edn, London: Thames and Hudson, 1975, pp. 181–182.
5. Frank Stella, *Working Space*, Cambridge, Mass.: Harvard University Press, 1986, p. 158.
6. ibid., p. 71.
7. Norbert Lynton, 'The Art Newspaper Interview: Frank Stella', *The Art Newspaper*, 94, July–August 1999, p. 67.
8. Hans Hofmann, *Search for the Real and Other Essays*, ed. Sara T. Weeks and Bartlett H. Hayes, Jr, Cambridge, Mass.: MIT Press, 1967, p. 67.
9. Pat Gilmour, *Innovation in Collaborative Printmaking: Kenneth Tyler 1963–1992* (exhibition catalogue), Tokyo: the Yomiuri Shimbun and the Japan Association of Art Museums, 1992, p. 168.
10. Frank Stella, 'Melrose Avenue', *Frank Stella at Tyler Graphics* (exhibition catalogue), Minneapolis: Walker Art Center, 1997, p. 33.
11. Robert Hughes, *Frank Stella: The Swan Engravings*, Fort Worth: Fort Worth Art Museum, 1984, p. 5.
12. Siri Engberg, 'Imaginary Places and the Art of the Everyday', in *Frank Stella at Tyler Graphics* (exhibition catalogue), Minneapolis: Walker Art Center, 1997, p. 10.
13. Ken Tyler, in *Reaching Out: Ken Tyler, master printer* (documentary film), Avery Tirce Productions, 1976.
14. Richard H. Axsom, *The Prints of Frank Stella: a catalogue raisonné 1967–1982*, New York: Hudson Hills Press, in association with the University of Michigan Museum of Art, Ann Arbor, 1983, cat. 1, p. 40.
15. Frank Stella, 'Melrose Avenue', in *Frank Stella at Tyler Graphics* (exhibition catalogue), Minneapolis: Walker Art Center, 1997, p. 39.
16. Interview with Christopher C. Cook, in *Frank Stella: from start to finish* (exhibition catalogue), Andover, Mass.: Addison Gallery of American Art, 1982.
17. Frank Stella, 'Melrose Avenue', in *Frank Stella and Kenneth Tyler: a unique 30-year collaboration* (exhibition catalogue), Fukushima: Center for Contemporary Graphic Art and the Tyler Graphics Archive Collection, 1998, p. 134.

18. ibid., p. 46.
19. Jacquelynn Baas, *Frank Stella: Moby Dick Deckle Edges*, Mount Kisco, New York: Tyler Graphics Ltd, 1993, p. 7.
20. Ken Tyler, correspondence with Jane Kinsman, 3 August 1999.
21. Jacquelynn Baas, *Frank Stella: Moby Dick Deckle Edges*, Mount Kisco, New York: Tyler Graphics Ltd, 1993, pp. 7–8. The relationship between text and image has been widely discussed, for example, in Philip Leider, 'Shakespearian Fish', *Art in America*, October 1990, pp. 172–91; Robert K. Wallace, *Frank Stella's Moby-Dick: words and shapes*, Ann Arbor: University of Michigan Press, 2000; and Pat Gilmour, 'Frank Stella's Moby Dick', *Print Quarterly*, 18(4) December 2001, pp. 414–436.
22. Ken Tyler, Qantas Birthday Lecture, 14 October 1999, National Gallery of Australia, Canberra.
23. ibid.
24. Ken Tyler, in *Frank Stella: Imaginary Places* (documentary film), Minneapolis: Walker Art Center, produced by Tyler Graphics, Mount Kisco, 1997.
25. Ken Tyler, correspondence with Jane Kinsman, 3 August 1999.
26. Ken Tyler, 'Notes on The Fountain', 13 January 1999, unpublished ms, National Gallery of Australia.
27. Ken Tyler, in *Frank Stella: Imaginary Places* (documentary film), Minneapolis: Walker Art Center, produced by Tyler Graphics, Mount Kisco, 1997. It is interesting to note that, for part of his career, Kandinsky also adopted the process of recycling for his abstractions.
28. ibid.
29. Ken Tyler, correspondence with Jane Kinsman, 5 July 1999.
30. Ken Tyler, 'Notes on The Fountain', 13 January 1999, unpublished ms,
31. Ken Tyler, Qantas Birthday Lecture, 14 October 1999, National Gallery of Australia, Canberra.
32. ibid.
33. Ken Tyler, in *Frank Stella: Imaginary Places* (documentary film), Minneapolis: Walker Art Center, produced by Tyler Graphics, Mount Kisco, 1997.

(above)
Frank STELLA
Çatal Hüyük (Level VI B) Shrine VIB.10 2001 cast aluminium and aluminium pipe (photograph by Steven Sloman, New York).

Catalogue

Unless otherwise stated, all works are in the collection of the National Gallery of Australia, Canberra. Measurements are given in centimetres, height, before width, before depth. Where two sizes are listed for the prints, composition precedes sheet size.

Josef ALBERS
Germany 1888 – United States of America 1976

Homage to the Square: On an Early Sky 1964
oil on composition board
122.2 x 122.2 cm
Purchased 1981 81.3043

from *White Line Squares* 1966
a boxed portfolio containing 17 colour
lithographs on Arches Cover mould-made paper
portfolio 53.2 x 53.6
slipcase 54.0 x 53.9
each lithograph 40.0 x 40.0 cm, 52.7 x 52.7 cm
right to print proofs, edition of 125
published by Gemini GEL, Los Angeles
Purchased 1973

    Series I: White Line Square I–VIII
    73.857.1–8

    Series II: White Line Square IX–XVI
    73.857.9–16

from *Gray Instrumentation II* 1975
a boxed portfolio with slipcase containing
12 colour screenprints on Arches 88 mould-made
paper with title, colophon, and 6 pages of verse
written by the artist
portfolio 50.9 x 50.9 cm, slipcase 52.0 x 51.4 cm
each screenprint 28.0 x 28.0 cm, 48.3 x 48.3 cm
right to print proofs, edition of 36
published by Tyler Workshop Ltd, Bedford
Village, New York Purchased 1975

    Gray Instrumentation IIc
    75.554.11

    Gray Instrumentation IIf
    75.554.14

    Gray Instrumentation IIg
    75.554.15

    Gray Instrumentation IIj
    75.554.18

Helen FRANKENTHALER
United States of America born 1928

Other Generations 1957
oil on canvas
174.7 x 177.9 cm
Purchased 1973 73.330

Hillside 1971
synthetic polymer paint on canvas
227.0 x 208.0 cm
Collection of Penelope and Harry Seidler

Java 1971
synthetic polymer paint on canvas
161.0 x 221.5 cm
Museum of Contemporary Art, Sydney

In the Meantime 1973
from *Thanksgiving Day*
a series of 71 ceramic tiles
stoneware with glazes
33.6 x 44.4 x 2.5 cm
Collection of Penelope and Harry Seidler

Essence Mulberry 1977
colour woodcut on buff Maniai gampi
handmade paper
101.0 x 47.0 cm
right to print proof, edition of 46
published by Tyler Graphics Ltd, Bedford Village,
New York
Purchased 1979 79.2871

Cameo 1980
colour woodcut on grey-pink
TGL handmade paper
107.0 x 81.6 cm
right to print proof, edition of 51
published by Tyler Graphics Ltd, Bedford Village,
New York
Purchased 1981 81.1009

Tiger's Eye 1987
colour aquatint, lithograph, etching, screenprint
47.6 x 55.9 cm
colour trial proof I/3, edition of 56
printed by Tyler Graphics Ltd, Mount Kisco,
New York
Gift of Kenneth Tyler 2002 2002.1.46

Tiger's Eye 1987
colour aquatint, lithograph, etching, screenprint
48.0 x 61.0 cm
colour trial proof III/3, edition of 56
printed by Tyler Graphics Ltd, Mount Kisco,
New York
Gift of Kenneth Tyler 2002 2002.1.47

Tiger's Eye 1987
colour aquatint, lithograph, etching, screenprint
on HMP handmade paper
48.5 x 57.0 cm
artist's proof 11/14, edition of 56
published by Tyler Graphics Ltd, Mount Kisco,
New York
Purchased with the assistance of the
Orde Poynton Fund 2002 2002.1.48

Gateway 1988
colour etching, relief, aquatint, stencil
on 3 sheets of TGL handmade paper
175.3 x 224.8 overall
artist's proof VI/10, edition of 30
published by Tyler Graphics Ltd, Mount Kisco,
New York
Purchased with the assistance of the
Orde Poynton Fund 2002 2002.1.63.A–C

Gateway (screen)
hand-patinated cast bronze in 3 panels
205.7 x 251.5 x 11.4 cm overall
trial proof II, edition of 12
Gift of Kenneth Tyler 2002 2002.1.90.A–C

Tales of Genji 1998
a series of 6 colour woodcuts, 4 with stencil
on coloured TGL handmade papers
published by Tyler Graphics Ltd, Mount Kisco,
New York
Purchased with the assistance of the
Orde Poynton Fund 2002 2002.1.78–83

    Tales of Genji I
    colour woodcut on light sienna
    TGL handmade paper
    106.7 x 119.4 cm
    3/30

Tales of Genji II
colour woodcut on pale orange
TGL handmade paper
119.4 x 106.7 cm
8/35

Tales of Genji III
colour woodcut, stencil on grey
TGL handmade paper
119.4 x 106.7 cm
3/36

Tales of Genji IV
colour woodcut, stencil on light rose
TGL handmade paper
119.4 x 106.7 cm
5/30

Tales of Genji V
colour woodcut, stencil on rust
TGL handmade paper
106.7 x 119.4 cm
3/36

Tales of Genji VI
colour woodcut, stencil on tan
TGL handmade paper
119.4 x 106.7 cm
3/35

David HOCKNEY
Great Britain born 1937,
working United States of America

A Hollywood Collection 1965
a series of 6 colour lithographs on Rives BFK paper
right to print proofs, edition of 85
printed by Kenneth Tyler, Gemini, Los Angeles
published by Editions Alecto, London
Purchased 1973 73.1049.1–6

**Picture of a Still Life that has an Elaborate
Silver Frame**
76.8 x 56.5 cm

**Picture of a Landscape in an Elaborate
Gold Frame**
76.9 x 56.6 cm

Picture of a Portrait in a Silver Frame
76.8 x 56.6 cm

**Picture of Melrose Avenue in an Ornate
Gold Frame**
76.8 x 56.6 cm

**Picture of a Simple Framed Traditional Nude
Drawing**
76.8 x 56.6 cm

**Picture of a Pointless Abstraction Framed
Under Glass**
76.9 x 56.6 cm

from *Weather* 1973
a series of 11 colour lithographs,
7 with screenprint
right to print proofs, edition of 98
published by Gemini GEL, Los Angeles
Purchased 1973

Rain
on Arches Cover mould-made paper
94.0 x 73.0 cm, 99.6 x 80.4 cm
73.1020

Sun
on Special Arjomari mould-made paper
76.8 x 64.2 cm, 94.8 x 77.8 cm
73.1021

Wind
on Special Arjomari mould-made paper
79.3 x 61.4 cm, 101.6 x 78.8 cm
73.1023

Lightning
on Special Arjomari mould-made paper
78.9 x 65.2 cm, 100.0 x 80.4 cm
73.1024

Mist
on Special Arjomari mould-made paper
74.0 x 64.0 cm, 94.2 x 81.2 cm
73.1025

Snow
on Special Arjomari mould-made paper
86.7 x 72.8 cm, 101.7 x 85.1 cm
73.1028

Celia 1973
lithograph on Angoumois à la main buff paper
92.1 x 68.2 cm, 108.7 x 73.1 cm
right to print proof, edition of 52
published by Gemini GEL, Los Angeles
Purchased 1973 73.1030

Celia, 8365 Melrose Avenue, Hollywood 1973
lithograph, crayon on Arches paper
87.4 x 77.3 cm, 121.7 x 80.5 cm
right to print proof, edition of 46
published by Gemini GEL, Los Angeles
Purchased 1973 73.1031

Celia Smoking 1973
lithograph on Angoumois à la main paper
98.8 x 72.6 cm
right to print proof, edition of 70
published by Gemini GEL, Los Angeles
Purchased 1973 73.1032

Celia in a Black Dress with Red Stockings 1973
coloured crayon drawing
64.8 x 49.5 cm
Gift of Orde Poynton Esq. CMG 1998 98.17

**The Master Printer of Los Angeles
[Portrait of Kenneth Tyler]** 1973
colour lithograph, screenprint on
Arches Cover paper
95.0 x 70.0 cm, 121.0 x 80.5 cm
right to print proof, edition of 27
published by Gemini GEL, Los Angeles
Purchased 1973 73.1034

Steps with Shadow, Paper Pool 2-H 1978
hand-coloured and pressed coloured paper pulp
130.0 x 86.8 cm
1 of 16 variations
published by Tyler Graphics Ltd, Bedford Village,
New York
Purchased 1979 79.2887

**Green Pool with Diving Board and Shadow,
Paper Pool 3-I** 1978
hand-coloured and pressed coloured paper pulp
128.8 x 82.1 cm
1 of 15 variations
published by Tyler Graphics Ltd, Bedford Village,
New York
Purchased 1979 79.2886

A Diver, Paper Pool 17 1978
on 12 sheets of hand-coloured and pressed
coloured paper pulp
182.8 x 434.3 cm overall
unique paper work
published by Tyler Graphics Ltd, Bedford Village,
New York
Purchased 1979 79.2343.1–12

Ken Tyler 1978
pen and sepia ink drawing
43.0 x 35.5 cm
Collection of David Hockney

**My Mother Sleeping, Los Angeles,
December 1982** 1982
photographic collage
58.1 x 58.1 cm
edition of 20
Collection of John Hockney

**Gregory Swimming, Los Angeles,
31 March 1982** 1982
composite polaroid
70.5 x 130.2 cm
Collection of David Hockney

Paint Trolley, L.A., 1985 1985
photographic collage
101.6 x 152.4 cm
1/1
Collection of David Hockney

from *Moving Focus* 1984–87
a series of 29 colour lithographs,
screenprint, etching, stencil, aquatint,
some with collage, handpainted frames,
published by Tyler Graphics Ltd, Bedford Village,
and Mount Kisco, New York

Amaryllis in Vase 1984
colour lithograph on TGL handmade paper
127.0 x 91.4 cm
trial proof III/9, edition of 80
Gift of Kenneth Tyler 2002
2002.1.51

**Pembroke Studio with Blue Chairs
and Lamp** 1985
colour lithograph on HMP handmade paper
47.0 x 55.9 cm
5/98
Purchased with the assistance of the
Orde Poynton Fund 2002 2002.1.88

Two Pembroke Studio Chairs 1984
colour lithograph on HMP handmade paper
47.0 x 55.9 cm
5/98
Purchased with the assistance of the
Orde Poynton Fund 2002 2002.1.87

Pembroke Studio Interior 1984
colour lithograph on TGL handmade paper,
hand-painted frame
102.9 x 125.7 cm, 117.2 x 140.0 cm
printer's proof I/2, edition of 70
Purchased with the assistance of the
Orde Poynton Fund 2002 2002.1.91

Tyler Dining Room 1985
colour lithograph on TGL handmade paper
81.2 x 101.5 cm
98/98
Purchased 1986 86.1865

Views of Hotel Well I 1984
colour lithograph on TGL handmade paper
79.4 x 105.4 cm
trial proof III/4, edition of 75
Gift of Kenneth Tyler 2002 2002.1.86

Views of Hotel Well II 1985
colour lithograph on HMP handmade paper
63.5 x 81.3 cm
trial proof I/1, edition of 75
Gift of Kenneth Tyler 2002 2002.1.92

Views of Hotel Well III 1984–85
colour lithograph on TGL handmade paper
123.2 x 97.8 cm
artist's proof X/18, edition of 80
Purchased with the assistance of the
Orde Poynton Fund 2002 2002.1. 93

Hotel, Acatlán: Second Day 1984–85
colour lithograph on 2 sheets of TGL
handmade paper
73.8 x 194.0 cm overall
right to print proof, edition of 98
Purchased 1986 86.1867.A–B

An Image of Gregory 1984–85
colour lithograph, collage on 2 sheets of
TGL handmade, St. Armand handmade
and HMP handmade paper
198.1 x 88.9 cm overall
trial proof II/5, edition of 75
Gift of Kenneth Tyler 2002 2002.1.59

Hotel, Acatlán: Two Weeks Later 1985
colour lithograph on 2 sheets of
HMP handmade paper
73.0 x 188.0 cm overall 2/98
Purchased with the assistance of the
Orde Poynton Fund 2002 2002.1.89.A–B

An Image of Celia 1986
colour lithograph, screenprint, collage on
TGL handmade, light tan TGL handmade
papers, and black German Etching mould-
made paper, hand-painted frame
151.1 x 104.1 cm, 168.9 x 121.0 cm
artist's proof XI/18, edition of 40
Purchased with the assistance of the
Orde Poynton Fund 2002 2002.1.94

An Image of Celia, State I 1984–86
colour lithograph on TGL handmade paper
125.7 x 99.1 cm
artist's proof V/6, edition of 10
Purchased with the assistance of the
Orde Poynton Fund 2002 2002.1.57

Walking Past Two Chairs 1984
colour lithograph, screenprint on
TGL handmade paper, hand-painted frame
55.9 x 100.3 cm, 71.2 x 116.2 cm
artist's proof XI/14, edition of 38
Purchased with the assistance of the
Orde Poynton Fund 2002 2002.1.95

Number One Chair 1985–86
colour lithograph, etching on HMP
handmade paper 55.9 x 47.6 cm
trial proof I, edition of 60
Gift of Kenneth Tyler 2002 2002.1.96

Number One Chair 1986
colour lithograph, etching on HMP
handmade paper 55.9 x 47.6 cm
trial proof III, edition of 60
Gift of Kenneth Tyler 2002 2002.1.97

Caribbean Tea Time 1987
colour lithograph, screenprint,
collage of Rives BFK surface-pigmented
paper, stencil on 8 sheets of TGL
handmade paper, in a 4-panel folding
lacquered wood screen,
hand-painted (verso),
with 4 screenprinted plastic panels (recto)
214.9 x 341.6 cm overall
artist's proof 9/10, edition of 36
published by Tyler Graphics Ltd,
Mount Kisco, New York
Purchased with the assistance of the
Orde Poynton Fund 2002 2002.1.98 A–D

Jasper JOHNS
United States of America born 1930

Color Numeral Series 1969
10 colour lithographs on Arjomari paper
right to print proofs, edition of 40
published by Gemini GEL, Los Angeles
Purchased 1973 73.884.1–10

Figure 0
70.6 x 56.4 cm, 97.2 x 79.2 cm

Figure 1
69.6 x 55.6 cm, 96.8 x 79.2 cm

Figure 2
70.2 x 55.4 cm, 96.8 x 79.2 cm

Figure 3
70.0 x 53.6 cm, 96.6 x 79.0 cm

Figure 4
69.4 x 54.6 cm, 96.8 x 79.6 cm

Figure 5
69.8 x 57.4 cm, 96.8 x 79.6 cm

Figure 6
70.6 x 54.0 cm, 97.2 x 79.4 cm

Figure 7
70.8 x 54.6 cm, 96.8 x 79.0 cm

Figure 8
72.2 x 57.0 cm, 96.8 x 79.2 cm

Figure 9
72.2 x 56.4 cm, 96.8 x 79.2 cm

No 1969
colour lithograph, embossing, collage of lead
letters on Arjomari paper 142.1 x 88.8 cm
right to print proof, edition of 90
published by Gemini GEL, Los Angeles
Purchased 1973 73.1056

Lead Reliefs 1969
a series of 5 lead reliefs
right to print proofs, edition of 60
published by Gemini GEL, Los Angeles
Purchased 1973 73.1057–1061

High School Days
sheet lead and glass mirror relief
59.1 x 44.0 cm

The Critic Smiles
sheet lead, gold casting and tin leafing relief
59.0 x 43.8 cm

Flag
sheet lead relief
43.9 x 59.2 cm

Light Bulb
sheet lead relief
99.5 x 43.8 cm

Bread
cast lead, sheet lead, paper and oil paint relief
58.4 x 43.2 cm

Numerals 1970
lead relief
76.6 x 60.0 cm
right to print proof, edition of 60
published by Gemini GEL, Los Angeles
Purchased 1973 73.1062

from *Fragments — According to What* 1971
a series of 6 colour lithographs on Arches Cover
mould-made and Crisbrook handmade papers
right to print proofs
published by Gemini GEL, Los Angeles
Purchased 1973 73.883.1–3

**Fragment — According to What:
Bent "Blue"**
colour lithograph with newspaper monotype
on Arches Cover mould-made paper
64.6 x 73.4 cm edition of 66

**Fragment — According to What:
Leg and Chair**
colour lithograph on Arches Cover
mould-made paper
90.0 x 75.6 cm edition of 68

**Fragment — According to What:
Coathanger and Spoon**
colour lithograph on Arches Cover
mould-made paper
87.2 x 64.6 cm edition of 76

Roy LICHTENSTEIN
United States of America 1923–1997

Kitchen Stove 1961–62
oil on canvas
173.0 x 173.0 cm
Purchased 1978 79.68

Peanut Butter Cup 1962
oil on canvas
35.5 x 35.5 cm
Collection of John Kaldor

Crak! 1963–64
colour lithograph
47.1 x 68.6 cm
outside the numbered edition of 300
published by Leo Castelli Gallery, New York
Purchased 1996 97.36

Kiss V 1964
oil on canvas
91.5 x 91.5 cm
Collection of Charles Simonyi

Shipboard Girl 1965
colour lithograph
66.6 x 49.0 cm, 69.0 x 51.4 cm
edition unknown
published by Leo Castelli Gallery, New York
Purchased 1972 72.509.245

Brushstroke 1967
colour screenprint
55.6 x 76.3 cm, 58.5 x 98.8 cm
189/300
published by Leo Castelli Gallery, New York
Purchased 1983 83.1472

from *Cathedral Series* 1969
8 colour lithographs on Special Arjomari paper
right to print proofs
published by Gemini GEL, Los Angeles
Purchased 1973

Cathedral #2
106.2 x 68.8 cm, 122.7 x 82.5 cm
edition of 75
73.899.2

Cathedral #4
106.2 x 68.8 cm, 123.2 x 82.5 cm
edition of 75
73.899.5

Cathedral #5
106.2 x 68.8 cm, 123.2 x 82.5 cm
edition of 75
73.899.6

Cathedral #6, State I
106.2 x 68.8 cm, 123.2 x 82.5 cm
edition of 13
73.899.3

from *Haystack Series* 1969
10 colour lithographs, some with screenprint
6 on Rives BFK paper, 4 on Special Arjomari
paper as indicated
right to print proofs
published by Gemini GEL, Los Angeles
Purchased 1973

Haystack #1
colour lithograph, screenprint
34.0 x 59.7 cm, 52.7 x 77.6 cm
edition of 100
73.905.1

Haystack #3
colour lithograph, screenprint
34.3 x 59.7 cm, 52.7 x 78.1 cm
edition of 100
73.905.3

Haystack #5
colour lithograph, screenprint
34.1 x 59.7 cm, 52.4 x 78.1 cm
edition of 100
73.905.5

Haystack #6
colour lithograph
34.1 x 59.7 cm, 52.4 x 78.1 cm
edition of 100
73.905.6

Haystack #6, State I
colour lithograph on Special Arjomari paper
34.1 x 59.7 cm, 52.4 x 78.1 cm
edition of 13
73.905.7

Haystack #6, State III
colour lithograph on Special Arjomari paper
34.1 x 59.7 cm, 52.4 x 78.1 cm
edition of 13
73.905.9

Peace Through Chemistry I 1970
colour lithograph, screenprint
on Special Arjomari paper
81.1 x 146.2 cm, 96.0 x 161.3 cm
right to print proof, edition of 32
published by Gemini GEL, Los Angeles
Purchased 1973 73.900.1

Untitled Head I 1970
brass
65.6 x 26.0 x 15.0 cm
right to print proof, edition of 75
published by Gemini GEL, Los Angeles
Purchased 1973 73.901.1

Untitled Head II 1970
California English walnut
77.6 x 30.6 cm x 33.6 cm diameter
right to print proof, edition of 30
published by Gemini GEL, Los Angeles
Purchased 1973 73.901.2

Peace Through Chemistry Bronze 1970
cast bronze relief
69.5 x 117.5 x 3.5 cm
9/38
published by Gemini GEL, Los Angeles
Purchased 1973 73.902

from *Modern Head* 1970
a series of 5 mixed-media prints
right to print proofs, edition of 100
published by Gemini GEL, Los Angeles
Purchased 1973 73.904.2–5

Modern Head #2
colour lithograph, linecut, embossing on
black handmade Waterleaf paper
50.3 x 29.8 cm, 61.0 x 46.4 cm

Modern Head #3
zinc linecut, embossing on black handmade
Waterleaf paper
50.8 x 35.5 cm, 61.0 x 46.0 cm

Modern Head #4
colour lithograph, engraved, anodised
aluminium and printed aluminium,
aluminium frame
52.7 x 43.8 cm

Modern Head #5
embossed graphite with Strathmore die-cut
paper overlay on anodised aluminium with
wood and enamelled aluminium frame
71.1 x 49.5 cm

Modern Head Relief 1970
brass
61.0 x 45.0 x 1.9 cm
32/100
published by Gemini GEL, Los Angeles

Chem 1A 1970
colour screenprint on Special Arjomari paper
61.0 x 36.4 cm, 76.2 x 51.6 cm
right to print proof, edition of 100
published by Gemini GEL, Los Angeles
Purchased 1973 73.907

Bull Profile 1973
a series of 7 mixed-media prints
on Arjomari paper
right to print proofs
published by Gemini GEL, Los Angeles
Purchased 1973 73.895.1–7

Bull I
linecut
51.3 x 74.9 cm, 68.8 x 88.9 cm
edition of 100

Bull II
colour lithograph, linecut
58.2 x 83.8 cm, 68.8 x 88.9 cm
edition of 100

Bull III
colour lithograph, screenprint, linecut
61.1 x 81.4 cm, 68.8 x 88.9 cm
edition of 100

Bull IV
colour lithograph, screenprint, linecut
59.6 x 85.4 cm, 68.8 x 88.9 cm
edition of 100

Bull V
colour lithograph, screenprint, linecut
59.6 x 85.2 cm, 68.8 x 88.9 cm
edition of 100

Bull VI
colour lithograph, screenprint, linecut
63.6 x 83.8 cm, 68.8 x 88.9 cm
edition of 100

Bull VII
colour lithograph, screenprint, linecut
61.0 x 83.8 cm, 68.8 x 88.9 cm
edition of 26

from *Entablatures* 1976
a series of 11 prints on Rives BFK paper,
collage, embossing
right to print proofs
published by Tyler Graphics Ltd, Bedford Village,
New York
Purchased 1976

Entablature II
colour screenprint, lithograph,
metal foil collage, embossing
50.2 x 96.6 cm, 74.2 x 114.2 cm
edition of 30
76.1535.2

Entablature III
colour screenprint, lithograph,
metal foil collage, embossing
52.6 x 96.6 cm, 74.2 x 114.2 cm
edition of 16
76.1535.3

Entablature V
colour screenprint, lithograph,
metal foil collage, embossing
55.4 x 96.6 cm, 74.2 x 114.2 cm
edition of 30
76.1535.5

Entablature X
colour screenprint, lithograph,
metal foil collage, embossing
53.4 x 96.6 cm, 74.2 x 114.2 cm
edition of 18
76.1535.10

Brushstroke VI 1986
from *Brushstroke Sculptures*, a series of
6 handpainted cherry wood sculptures
152.4 x 147.3 x 25.4 cm
8/10
published by Tyler Graphics Ltd, Bedford Village,
New York
Collection of Penelope and Harry Seidler

Brushstroke Contest 1989
colour lithograph on Rives BFK paper
127.0 x 101.6 cm
printer's proof 1/2, edition of 36
published by Tyler Graphics Ltd, Mount Kisco,
New York
Purchased with the assistance of the
Orde Poynton Fund 2002 2002.1.60

Brushstroke on Canvas 1989
colour lithograph on Rives BFK paper
95.9 x 92.1 cm
artist's proof 12/18, edition of 40
published by Tyler Graphics Ltd, Mount Kisco,
New York
Purchased with the assistance of the
Orde Poynton Fund 2002 2002.1.61

from *Reflections* 1989–90
a series of 7 colour lithographs, screenprint,
woodcut, metalised PVC plastic film collage,
embossing on mould-made Somerset papers
edition of 68
published by Tyler Graphics Ltd, Mount Kisco,
New York

Reflections on Hair
142.6 x 114.3 cm
artist's proof 14/16
Purchased with the assistance of the
Orde Poynton Fund 2002 2002.1.84

Reflections on Conversation
136.5 x 169.9 cm
artist's proof 14/16
Purchased with the assistance of the
Orde Poynton Fund 2002 2002.1.73

Reflections on Crash
150.2 x 190.5 cm
53/68
Purchased 1991 91.106

Reflections on The Scream
123.8 x 166.1 cm
4/68
Purchased with the assistance of the
Orde Poynton Fund 2002 2002.1.76

Reflections on Brushstrokes
145.0 x 180.3 cm
artist's proof 14/16
Purchased with the assistance of the
Orde Poynton Fund 2002 2002.1.72

Reflections on Girl
114.6 x 139.1 cm
1/68
Purchased with the assistance of the
Orde Poynton Fund 2002 2002.1.74

Reflections on Minerva
106.7 x 131.4 cm
artist's proof 14/16
Purchased with the assistance of the
Orde Poynton Fund 2002 2002.1.75

from *Nudes* 1994
a series of 9 colour relief prints
published by Tyler Graphics Ltd, Mount Kisco,
New York
Purchased with the assistance of the
Orde Poynton Fund 2002

Nude with Blue Hair
146.7 x 93.5 cm
1/40
2002.1.70

Nude with Yellow Pillow
133.8 x 109.2 cm
right to print proof, edition of 60
2002.1.71

Roommates
163.2 x 129.5 cm
right to print proof, edition of 40
2002.1.77

Robert MOTHERWELL
United States of America 1915–1991

Elegy to the Spanish Republic 1958
synthetic polymer paint on canvas
175.3 x 248.9 cm
Daedalus Foundation through the American
Friends of the Australian National Gallery 1994
94.1

Bastos 1974–75
colour lithograph on Arjomari paper
158.4 x 101.0 cm
right to print proof, edition of 49
published by Tyler Graphics Ltd, Bedford Village,
New York
Purchased 1975 75.556

Monster 1975
colour lithograph on speckled grey
HMP handmade paper
103.0 x 78.5 cm
right to print proof, edition of 26
published by Tyler Graphics Ltd, Bedford Village,
New York
Purchased 1975 75.558

St Michael III 1979
colour lithograph, screenprint
on mottled grey HMP handmade paper
105.4 x 83.0 cm
right to print proof, edition of 99
published by Tyler Graphics Ltd, Bedford Village,
New York
Purchased 1979 79.2893

Lament for Lorca 1982
lithograph
111.4 x 154.0 cm
unsigned proof, edition of 52
printed by Tyler Graphics, Bedford Village,
New York
Gift of Kenneth Tyler 2002 2002.1.29.1

El Negro
a bound book of 17 original lithographs
illuminating the Rafael Alberti poem
El Negro Motherwell, in a case covered
with natural buckram cloth
published by Tyler Graphics Ltd, Bedford Village,
New York, 1983
colour lithograph, letterpress on
TGL handmade paper
39.2 x 38.0 cm
trial proof 1/1, edition of 51
Gift of Kenneth Tyler 2002 2002.1.62

El Negro
a bound book of 17 original lithographs
illuminating the Rafael Alberti poem
El Negro Motherwell, in a case covered
with natural buckram cloth
published by Tyler Graphics Ltd, Bedford Village,
New York, 1983
colour lithograph, letterpress on
TGL handmade paper
39.2 x 38.0 cm
right to print proof, edition of 51
Purchased 1983 83.2921.1–21

from *America-La France Variations* 1983–84
a series of 9 colour lithographs, collage on
TGL handmade paper, unless indicated
published by Tyler Graphics Ltd, Bedford Village,
New York

America-La France Variations I
118.1 x 81.6 cm 66/70
Purchased with the assistance of the
Orde Poynton Fund 2002 2002.1.85

America-La France Variations II
115.6 x 73.7 cm 2/70
Purchased with the assistance of the
Orde Poynton Fund 2002 2002.1.55

America-La France Variations III
on black Arches Cover paper
121.9 x 78.1 cm 2/70
Purchased with the assistance of the
Orde Poynton Fund 2002 2002.1.56

America-La France Variations V
on Arches Cover paper
116.8 x 80.0 cm
right to print proof, edition of 60
Purchased 1985 85.1114

Blue Elegy 1987
colour relief, lithograph on TGL handmade,
hand-coloured paper
105.4 x 146.7 cm
artist's proof VIII/12, edition of 30
published by Tyler Graphics Ltd, Mount Kisco,
New York
Purchased with the assistance of the
Orde Poynton Fund 2002 2002.1.99

Burning Elegy 1991
colour lithograph, hand-coloured on
TGL handmade, hand-coloured paper
133.4 x 160.7 cm
artist's proof 1/12, edition of 36
published by Tyler Graphics Ltd, Mount Kisco,
New York
Purchased with the assistance of the
Orde Poynton Fund 2002 2002.1.100

Mediterranean Light 1991
colour lithograph on TGL handmade paper
83.2 x 193.7 cm
trial proof I/3, edition of 40
Gift of Kenneth Tyler 2002 2002.1.67

Mediterranean Light 1991
colour lithograph on TGL handmade,
hand-coloured paper
83.2 x 193.7 cm
16/40
published by Tyler Graphics Ltd, Mount Kisco,
New York
Purchased with the assistance of the
Orde Poynton Fund 2002 2002.1.69

Robert RAUSCHENBERG
United States of America born 1925

from *Booster and 7 Studies* a series of 9 colour
lithographs, 1 with screenprint
published by Gemini GEL Los Angeles
Purchased 1973

Booster 1967
colour lithograph, screenprint
on Curtis Rag machine-made paper
183.0 x 89.0 cm
right to print proof, edition of 38
73.927

from *Stoned Moon* 1969–70
a series of 33 colour lithographs,
1 with screenprint
published by Gemini GEL, Los Angeles
Purchased 1973

Horn 1969
on Special Rives paper
105.0 x 86.2 cm
right to print proof, edition of 58
73.1157

Sack 1969
on Special Arjomari paper
101.7 x 71.0 cm
right to print proof, edition of 60
73.1161

Banner 1969
on Special Arjomari paper
137.2 x 91.4 cm
right to print proof, edition of 40
73.1163

Waves 1969
on Special Arjomari paper
225.6 x 106.6 cm
right to print proof, edition of 27
73.943

Sky Garden 1969
on Special Arjomari paper
226.2 x 106.7 cm
colour trial proof, edition of 35
73.945

Sky Garden 1969
on Special Arjomari paper
225.9 x 106.4 cm
right to print proof, edition of 35
73.944

Tracks 1970
on Special Arjomari paper
111.6 x 88.8 cm
right to print proof, edition of 54
73.1166

Hybrid 1970
on Special Arjomari paper
138.4 x 91.2 cm
right to print proof, edition of 52
73.1170

Local Means 1970
on Special Arjomari paper
81.8 x 109.7 cm
right to print proof, edition of 11
73.1171

from *Pages and Fuses* 1973–74, a series of
12 coloured paper pulp works with collage
published by Gemini GEL, Los Angeles
Purchased 1975

Link 1974
a paper pulp work, pigment, collage
of screenprinted tissue
60.4 x 49.4 cm
right to print proof, edition of 29
75.610

Frank STELLA
United States of America born 1936

Flin Flon 1970
synthetic polymer and fluorescent paint
on canvas
274.0 x 274.0 cm
Purchased with the assistance of
Terrey and Anne Arcus and
Penelope and Harry Seidler 2002 2002.294

from *Newfoundland* 1971
a series of 6 colour lithographs, 2 with
screenprint on Special Arjomari papers
right to print proofs
published by Gemini GEL, Los Angeles
Purchased 1973 73.957.1–4

River of Ponds I
96.6 x 96.6 cm
edition of 78

River of Ponds II
96.5 x 96.5 cm
edition of 78

River of Ponds III
96.4 x 96.7 cm
edition of 75

River of Ponds IV
96.6 x 96.7 cm
edition of 70

from *Circuits* 1982–84
a series of 16 mixed-media prints
published by Tyler Graphics Ltd, Bedford Village,
New York

Pergusa Three 1982
colour relief, woodcut on TGL handmade,
hand-coloured paper
167.6 x 132.1 cm
colour trial proof 4/5, edition of 30
printed by Tyler Graphics Ltd, Bedford
Village, New York
Gift of Kenneth Tyler 2002 2002.1.101.1

Pergusa Three 1982
colour relief, woodcut on TGL handmade,
hand-coloured paper
167.6 x 132.1 cm
colour trial proof 5/5, edition of 30
printed by Tyler Graphics Ltd, Bedford
Village, New York
Gift of Kenneth Tyler 2002 2002.1.101.2

Pergusa Three 1983
colour relief, woodcut
on TGL handmade, hand-coloured paper
167.6 x 132.1 cm
artist's proof 12/18, edition of 30
Purchased with the assistance of the
Orde Poynton Fund 2002 2002.1.101.3

Imola Three, State II 1984
colour relief, woodcut
on TGL handmade, hand-coloured paper
167.6 x 132.1 cm
1/30
Purchased with the assistance of the
Orde Poynton Fund 2002 2002.1.64

Pergusa Three Double 1984
colour relief, screenprint, woodcut, engraving
on 2 sheets of TGL handmade,
hand-coloured paper
259.1 x 167.6 cm overall
right to print proof, edition of 30
Gift of Ken and Lindsay Tyler through the
American Friends of the Australian National
Gallery 1985 85.2025

dome-shaped magnesium plate for
Jonah Historically Regarded (Dome) 1992
100 cm diameter
Gift of Kenneth Tyler 2002 2002.1.103

dome-shaped magnesium plate for
The Cabin: Ahab and Starbuck (Dome) 1992
100 cm diameter
Gift of Kenneth Tyler 2002 2002.1.104

from *Moby Dick Domes* 1992
a series of 5 colour etchings, aquatint,
relief, engraving, 1 with screenprint, stencil,
hand-coloured
published by Tyler Graphics Ltd, Mount Kisco,
New York

Jonah Historically Regarded (Dome)
colour etching, aquatint, relief, engraving,
screenprint, stencil, hand-coloured on shaped
TGL handmade paper
186.7 x 134.6 x 15.2 cm
artist's proof 5/6, edition of 21
Purchased with the assistance of the
Orde Poynton Fund 2002 2002.1.105

The Cabin: Ahab and Starbuck (Dome)
colour etching, aquatint, relief, engraving
on shaped TGL handmade paper
185.4 x 134.6 x 15.2 cm
trial proof II/3, edition of 20
Gift of Kenneth Tyler 2002 2002.1.106

The Fountain 1992
colour woodcut, etching, aquatint, relief,
drypoint, screenprint, collage, hand-coloured
on 3 sheets of natural handmade, hand-coloured
triple-layered kozo fibre and handmade natural
gampi fibre
231.1 x 700.4 cm overall
4/8
published by Tyler Graphics Ltd, Mount Kisco,
New York
Gift of Orde Poynton Esq. CMG 1999 99.2.1–3

from *Moby Dick Deckle Edges* 1993
a series of 10 colour lithographs, some with
etching, aquatint, relief, engraving, screenprint,
collagraph or mezzotint
edition of 32
published by Tyler Graphics Ltd, Mount Kisco,
New York
Gift of Kenneth Tyler 2002

Ambergris 1993
colour lithograph, etching, aquatint,
relief, engraving, screenprint
on TGL handmade paper
106.0 x 133.4 cm
trial proof III/12
2002.1.54

Ambergris 1993
colour lithograph, etching, aquatint,
relief, engraving, screenprint
on TGL handmade paper
106.0 x 133.4 cm
trial proof V/12
2002.1.53

Ambergris 1993
colour lithograph, etching, aquatint,
relief, engraving, screenprint
on TGL handmade paper
106.0 x 133.4 cm
trial proof XII/12
2002.1.52

printing matrix for **Juam** 1997
carved plywood base with 102 irregularly
shaped elements (1 honeycomb aluminium,
39 copper and 12 magnesium plates,
11 poured aluminium, 16 brass and
1 bronze elements, 22 aluminium rings)
and 3 irregularly shaped plastic and
1 aluminium non-printing mask plates
207.3 x 160.0 x 3.2 cm
Gift of Kenneth Tyler 2002 2002.1.102

from *Imaginary Places* 1994–97
a series of 15 mixed-media prints
published by Tyler Graphics Ltd, Mount Kisco,
New York
Purchased with the assistance of the
Orde Poynton Fund 2002

Juam 1997
colour relief, etching, aquatint, lithograph,
screenprint, woodcut, engraving on 2 sheets
of TGL handmade, hand-coloured paper
207.3 x 160.0 cm overall
artist's proof 9, edition of 40
2002.1.65.A–B

Juam, State I 1997
colour relief, woodcut, etching, aquatint,
hand-coloured on TGL handmade,
hand-coloured paper
198.8 x 152.4 cm
artist's proof 5, edition of 16
2002.1.66

Çatal Hüyük (Level VI B) Shrine VIB.10 2001
cast aluminium and aluminium pipe
228.6 x 228.6 x 228.6 cm
Collection of Frank Stella

Mersin XVI 2001
mixed media on cast aluminium
193.0 x 188.0 cm
Collection of Kenneth and Marabeth Tyler

*The Big Americans: Albers, Frankenthaler,
Hockney, Johns, Lichtenstein, Motherwell,
Rauschenberg, Stella at Tyler's studios*

National Gallery of Australia, Canberra
4 October 2002 – 27 January 2003

Catalogue compiled by Roy Forward,
National Gallery of Australia

Index